AND GOD WHISPERED...
A MESSAGE FOR OUR TIME

BOOK I – THE CALL TO ONENESS
WITH A SEVEN WEEK PROCESS FOR SPIRITUAL AWAKENING

Revised Edition

ERNIE PAPPA

Copyright © 2024 by Ernie Pappa.

ISBN: 979-8-89465-062-3 (sc)
ISBN: 979-8-89465-063-0 (e)

All rights reserved. No part of this publication may be reproduced, distributed, or transmitted in any form or by any means, including photocopying, recording, or other electronic or mechanical methods, without the prior written permission of the author, except in the case of brief quotations embodied in critical reviews and certain other noncommercial uses permitted by copyright law.

This is a work of fiction. Characters, names, places, businesses, incidents, and events are either the products of the author's imagination or used in a fictitious manner. Any resemblance to actual persons, living or dead, or actual events is purely coincidental.

Printed in the United States of America.

Integrity Publishing
39343 Harbor Hills Blvd Lady Lake,
FL 32159

www.integrity-publishing.com

FROM THE AUTHOR

Through prayer, contemplation, meditation, and other spiritual practices early in life I discovered my inner connection with God and the Spirit within. I was able to allow the power of Oneness Consciousness that pervades the Universe and all of Creation, to direct my life. After some years, I learned to tap into my Spirit while fully conscious and conducting my everyday activities of life. The gentle urges of Spirit felt like 'Whispers' that countered the ego urges that often direct us into worldly and harmful actions. Rather, the 'Whispers' of Spirit provided Truths and Wisdom that nurtured my spiritual growth.

I have been urged by Spirit to share these 'Whispers' with the world so that others can better follow the urging and flow of their Spirit into a life of spiritual growth through contemplative prayer, meditation, truth, and wisdom. The 'Whispers' found in this book are powerful tools for anyone who sincerely desires to live according to their life mission and to bring Spirit into everyday life so that they can live in harmony with the Oneness Consciousness of all Creation.

HOW TO READ THIS BOOK

Relax and put yourself in an open receptive state. As you read, listen to the truths as if they were being whispered in your right ear and to your heart. You will find that, even if you cannot relax at first, the 'Whispers' will relax you. You will feel loved, cared for and blessed.

The 'whispered truths' will change your life if you allow them to enter your consciousness without judgment or criticism. If you are open, as a child is open and receptive, the truths will take on a special meaning that is uniquely your own.

This book is presented in a free-flowing style that will minimize critical thinking but will touch your heart and engage your intuition. Overly intellectual people may have difficulty connecting with this style of communication unless they are capable of being open and sincere in their approach to spiritual growth. They will need to put their critical mind aside and simply read and listen with a child's heart. Whoever is drawn to experience these 'Whispers' will have the opportunity to be transformed by the spiritual content within them.

Spiritual life is not linear or sequential. One may start anywhere and radiate within and without in growth and progress. One always starts where one is. There are no prerequisites. One just begins. Remember, if you weren't meant to find the truth, you would not have had the urge to live spiritually; nor would you have been led to this book.

My wish is that in reading 'And God Whispered...' and feeling its content within your Being, you will receive something useful for your journey and learn to follow the flow of your Spirit.

CONTENTS

Beginning Prayer..................................ix
Prayer & Meditation............................... x
Introduction – "Come into the silence and drink
 from the well of truth..."............ xii
Chapter 1 – "You are my child made from
 my cosmic light".................... 1
Chapter 2 – "This is the message for your time...
 awake, my child, awake"............... 6
Chapter 3 – "Dive deeply into the well of
 my consciousness"................... 12
Chapter 4 – "Believe in me, not the world".......... 20
Chapter 5 – "This is your call".................... 26
Chapter 6 – "Where you go when you die".......... 32
Chapter 7 – "You are the only you that you are"...... 40
Chapter 8 – "My universe is constantly recreated
 through change".................... 46
Chapter 9 – "Open yourself to my ordination"....... 54
Chapter 10 – "You can come to me in many ways".... 60
Chapter 11 – "Follow the flow of your Spirit"........ 70
Chapter 12 – "This is how my universe works"....... 78
Chapter 13 – "This is what keeps you from me"...... 84

Chapter 14 – "Live In your Being" 92
Chapter 15 – "Choose the energy that will
                lead you to me" 98
Chapter 16 – "When you believe you know…
                that's all you know" 108
Chapter 17 – "Discern organizational and religious
                limitations that obstruct you from
                entering the inner kingdom" 114
Chapter 18 – "I have looked into my churches
                and this is what I have seen…" 122
Chapter 19 – "The one change that will change
                everything" 128
Chapter 20 – "Everything you do…
                do with a full heart" 134
Chapter 21 – "Stop the chatter…learn to live
                in the quiet recesses of your Being" 138
Chapter 22 – "This Dialogue Will Continue" 142
Appendix – A Seven Week Process
                For Spiritual Awakening 148
Some Final Thoughts 180

BEGINNING PRAYER

Beloved God open my heart and mind to your 'Whispers' so that I may tread on the path of goodness and joy that you make available to all beings that desire kinship with you. Spiritual Helpers and Angels of the celestial spheres; join in God's 'Whispers' with your guidance and protective energy to guard me from all negativity and error ridden thoughts. Help keep me in the light and wisdom that will lead me to my home in Oneness. Help me to receive all that I need to transcend the traps and pitfalls of material existence so that my thoughts and feelings always lean on truth, spiritual realities, peace, and harmony. Assist me in radiating love and kindness to all those that I encounter so that they may be awakened to your Divine Presence within. Amen.

PRAYER & MEDITATION

The two most powerful tools for spiritual growth and attaining closeness to God are prayer and meditation. Prayer and meditation work together to bring about substantial changes in the consciousness of one aspiring to grow spiritually.

Prayer, in its most basic form, is talking to God. What most people miss in this process, however, is that we need to listen for answers, which in this book are given in the form of 'Whispers'.

The same principle is at work in our communication with other people, if we talk and do not listen, we will soon find that we are devoid of friends because people want to be heard and responded to. So does God.

I call the most effective prayer 'Contemplative Prayer' because it seeks to provide guidance and answers from God. Such prayer always involves the heart. We can 'feel' God's presence when we pray in this way while seeking answers and clarifications for our life.

Meditation involves techniques for quieting the mind and creating a receptivity to the Divine. Meditation works very well with prayer in that it builds a fertile inner ground for receiving intuitive inspiration for our life.

Visualization is often used to take us to inner realities and landscapes that are illuminated with light and bliss.

This is the power of meditation; that it can transport us to realities in the celestial spheres within our own consciousness. In essence, one can experience a profound reality without having to take a step; one can travel to the heavens and walk with one foot in the celestial realms while living an otherwise normal 'appearing' life on earth.

In this book you will find unique Contemplative Prayers and Meditations after each chapter so that you will have the tools to employ the guidance you receive from the 'Whispers'. Additionally, you will be provided with Affirmations to enlighten your consciousness with objective suggestions that go along with the 'Whispers', and with Contemplative Prayers and Meditations that enable you to put into action a powerful spiritual routine for your journey.

"Come into the silence and drink from the well of truth..."

INTRODUCTION

What is the secret of creating a dialogue with God, or with highly evolved Beings often called Angels? There are countless stories of people being helped in times of danger or peril by such entities who appear to take our survival and well-being to heart and offer us guidance and assistance in our life.

The question is…how can we initiate and enhance such a relationship with God and the Universe? This book is an attempt to answer that question and more… to offer the guidance that I received over a period of many years. Guidance from the heart of God, a most benevolent Being, who always… always has our best interest as the center of His relationship with us.

All we need to do is become receptive to his promptings; to quiet ourselves from the frenetic, all-consuming thoughts of the world and learn to listen and 'feel' His presence within us. There are a number of ways to achieve this and many of them will be offered to the reader in the For Pondering, Contemplative Prayer, Meditation and Affirmation sections at the end of each chapter.

To become receptive, one needs to enter the deeper parts of one's consciousness and affirm positive thoughts.

This will feed more sensitive attributes that lie within the depths of our being that will become activated and bring about positive changes. A transformation from a worldly consciousness into a spiritual consciousness can then occur.

With practice; with listening; with choosing the spiritual side of one's being, one can follow Spirit while walking on the earth. When that occurs, one walks with one foot on the earth and the other in the celestial sphere of omnipresence. It is a matter of choosing to take the spiritual route rather than the earthly route. Many small choices for Spirit will result in the accomplishment of a fully conscious human being. One needs only begin.

This book can be a beginning for many readers!

And now, listen to God's voice and feel His presence within you.

And God Whispered...

"Come into the silence and drink from the well of truth which is available to all who venture beneath the stormy seas of restlessness, there we are one, there I will gently speak to your being, there I will give you instructions on becoming... on becoming who you truly are.

There I will teach you the forgotten way of joy, there I will show you the route back home, there I will give you the way to journey with me throughout all eternity, there I will help you experience your internal Oneness with me and all of creation. Oneness is the unified consciousness that replaces the dual conscious/subconscious that has been the normal way of being on earth.

I have sent many world teachers throughout the ages to lead humans back to the beginning impulse of each lifetime so that they could journey into my kingdom and continue on the ladder of divine unfoldment. A number of souls have been able to attain freedom from the shackles of earthly life because of these teachers, However, most humans missed the opportunity or were not ready to ascend.

It has been as it should have been but now the process is changing. Everything in the universe is determined by its level of vibrations. Energy vibrations proceed from the highest, finest energy transmitted directly from me and continually graded down to the coarsest energy found in the physical material realm. In humans, the harsher or coarser the thoughts, manifestations, and actions of a person, the lower is the level of that person's being. Those humans who can love with an open heart and tune into the truth within themselves represent higher levels of being.

Those who live within their ego are cut off or separated from me, from other humans and from higher energies within themselves. The planet earth has been steeped in lower, harsher, vibrations for many thousands of years but has been gradually permeated with higher levels of energy for the past several hundred years. Now earth is ready to receive a new thrust of finer energies through the galactic system that I arranged when the universe was first formed. These higher vibrations will cause many world helpers to come forward who will be able to assist in accelerating the spiritual growth of everyone on the planet.

Those that have been consciously working throughout many lifetimes to attain freedom will now be able to awaken to Oneness. There will be many more consciously enlightened beings on the planet who will pass on finer vibrations to others, who ordinarily would have needed many more lifetimes to awaken. The entire process of conscious growth will be intensified and accelerated.

This is the foundation of a new higher age that has been foretold by many throughout time at my bidding. Human life on earth will be transformed, creating an entirely new civilization. Technology will speed up and new forms of energy will be discovered that will be freely available to all. Food production will change eradicating all hunger. Human society will recognize that all brother and sister humans are the greatest resources on the planet who will create ways to provide shelter, food and energy for all, thus removing poverty.

Spiritual growth and cultivation will become the central focus of all activity on earth. Conscious awareness will cause the wealthy to give their material resources to the greater needs of the world and they will let go of the drive to accumulate wealth, material goods, and power. No government or institution will dictate these changes…the changes will occur naturally out of a higher consciousness that will predominate.

This book is being presented from the well of divine truth and will assist all who are open…to recognize and avail themselves of higher transformative energies and processes that are actively evolving on the planet. On the other hand, those living in and holding onto the way of ego life will have much difficulty, for that way of life will come to an end and give way to the higher vibrational awareness of Oneness. Those who need to dominate and control will dwell in realms of lower vibrational energy when they leave the earth until they learn how to open to the truth that resides within themselves and raise their personal energy vibrations. Venture forward into what is being given to you and allow these truths to soak into your being.

Do not hold onto these truths with your intellect but rather learn to flow with your Spirit into your own discovery of truth within your Self. Be at peace, love others and stop trying to fix everyone and everything around you, for you may not have the answer yet, but you will receive the truth within yourselves... if you but tune into the new energy vibrations in on the planet. Accept and flow, and you will find yourself on the journey to higher levels of being. Allow what is being given to you within these pages to raise your vibrations and help you become receptive to higher levels of consciousness.

Be present to my divinity within yourself, open your heart and your consciousness, dive within your silence with me every day, Ponder the truths you encounter, and manage your life meeting the responsibilities you have been given. Everything will take its natural course as you ascend. Your life will become more joyous, blissful and successful in every way."

For Pondering

You have a treasure of spiritual wealth within you. You are a child of the Universe with riches beyond your wildest dreams. You have but to open the doorway to your Spirit, enter the inner realm beneath your ordinary consciousness, and tap into the Truth and Bliss within your Being.

Unfortunately, most people are so hypnotized by everything in the world; money, drama, career, relationships, materialism, power, politics, acquiring all kinds of things, etc. that they do not seek to explore their Divine nature within. They will run on the treadmill of life until they die and then continue to do so when they leave the planet.

In this Introduction, God leads us into some possibilities for inner exploration as He unfolds a new way of being for humans living in this Age. You, the reader, will be given the keys to true spirituality and shown how to unfold a life of joy and fulfillment that has the potential to take you out of the wheel of negative repetition. You will be given a ticket to higher realms of existence and learning. These 'Whispers' offer you the secrets of spiritual unfoldment perfectly expressed for our contemporary world.

Contemplative Prayer

Beloved God, I am your child made of your Spirit. Bring me into the joy of your all-encompassing Being. Allow me to feel your Presence and hear your Whispers so that I may be continually guided in my life here on earth and in Heaven after I leave this world. You are my light and my salvation now and forevermore. Keep my mind and heart within your Oneness in every moment.

Meditation

Relax and follow your breath in and out, feeling yourself as one with all of Creation. Creation is One and you are now in the vibration of Oneness, feeling joy and peace and love. Within this Oneness vibration lies the Truth. The longer you can keep yourself here, the more Truth you will experience. You are leaving separation and ego behind. In this state of Oneness, you are joining many others who are here and together you will build a new world of beneficial vibrations that will heal and bless others. Internally chant Om *(the primordial sound of the Divine)* at your Heart at the center of your chest, then at the point between your eyebrows and then at the top of your head. Continue to move from your Heart to the point between your eyebrows and then to the top of your head chanting Om until you are saturated with the joy of Oneness.

Affirmation

(Repeat Affirmations aloud first, then more and more quietly, then as a whisper, then silently within.)

My Being is an expression of the Oneness Consciousness that pervades all mineral, vegetable, animal, and human life in the Universe. I am One with all and radiate joy and peace always.

"You are my child made from my cosmic light"

CHAPTER 1

What is the purpose of life? Why are we here? What are we supposed to accomplish? Are we here to get a job and raise a family, or perhaps to become a famous actor or musician or author? Or to save lives in the medical field? Or to become a Minister or Priest or Guru? Or to learn what homelessness and addiction feel like? Truly there are many, many, many options… as many as there are people on earth.

In fact, each person chooses the way he or she lives in every moment, making choices that will lead to a positive fulfilling life or to a negative depleting one.

The interesting thing is…most people never even ponder the purpose of their life. Most humans just live on 'automatic' in a sort of sleep state that takes them to a destination that they never intended to reach. This is the main problem in ordinary human consciousness…the walking 'sleep' state. This book is about 'waking' from that sleep state and living in full consciousness while here and leaving the earth as an awake being. In such a condition one remains awake in the afterlife and will serve profoundly in the heavenly realms.

Let us continue with God's guidance for living a fully awakened life:

And God Whispered…

"You are my child. What true parent wants anything but good for his or her children? I want you to live in joy and to have what you need, to become a co-creator of the universe with me. There is no limit to what you can do, know that you can access everything you require right where you are…within your own Being. I am the well of positive energy that created you, that created everything. I am Creation. You are my child made from my light. You can do anything you wish if you but access me within yourself, if you but become realized in my Oneness, if you but live in the Spirit within your Being. Wherever you are in your life, whatever beliefs you have, whatever impulses drive your desires… you can begin to swim within my joy. Come to me within the silence, and I will teach you the way of truth, the way of love. In the pool of my love and joy and truth you will begin to heal, you will feel comfort, you will awaken, you will begin to walk in the Spirit with me, you will flow in your life easily and smoothly without obstruction.

Because within me there is clarity… no obstruction, no limitation, and my way shall be your way. The more deeply you drink of my cleansing waters of truth…Truth is reality; exactly what is…Truth is undeniable and free from all interpretation, all opinion, free from all merely intellectual.

Drink from my waters of truth and you will realize who and what you truly are. Dive deeply my child. Every day come to me. Dive into the ocean of my bliss, grow into my being…

And you shall bless the world with light and love."

For Pondering

Most people are so attached to earthly life, to their body, to their ordinary mind and emotions that they never, even for a moment, consider that they are children of God. If we can truly grasp that we are Divine in nature with God and the Universe as our real parents and ancestry, things would be very different for our life. We could gain the ability to identify less with body, mind and emotions and become more able to express our Divine universal nature... our Oneness. We would then be able to let go of our ego-separate existence that creates tension, stress, and unhappiness in our lives and ultimately in the world. When we are able to live in our universal Oneness consciousness, we will be able to feel creation in our midst as well as the Divine nature of everyone around us.

Contemplative Prayer

Heavenly Father, creator of all that is. My wish is to live within your presence in each moment. Strengthen my connection to Your Divine nature and give me the joy of being one of your ministers on earth. Help me to spread your joy and good will as I journey through life. Thank you for the blessed impulse to live within you.

Meditation

Relax and follow your breath in...and...out, feeling yourself as one with all of Creation. You were born in a body, but you are a child of the Universe. All children, though having an earthly father and mother are from Divine essence, from the essence of Spirit and Creation. Dive deeply into that part of yourself within that knows and feels the Truth of all of Creation. Feel the Oneness of Truth within...feel the flow of your Spirit. In this way, you will grow within the Being of Creation and be untouched by the harmful effects of the world. Focus on the center of your Being, at the Heart Center in the middle of your chest and internally chant Om...Om...Om...for as long as you feel the need to remain within Creation, within Spirit, within Oneness.

Affirmation

I am diving deeply into the well of Truth within my Being. There I will find the answers to all of life's questions and challenges. There I become one with Spirit. The more I dwell within, the more I become what I truly am as a Divine Child of the Universe.

"This is the message for your time... awake, my child, awake"

CHAPTER 2

To awaken is to become aware of your real identity as Spirit. When you believe you are only a body, you are asleep. When you understand and 'feel' yourself as Spirit, you are on the path to becoming a true human being that is awakened. True human beings have a special place in the heavenly spheres after leaving earth. As a true human being, living in Spirit, you will continue to learn and grow in the afterlife and be able to make real contributions to the spiritual unfoldment of the Universe. In other words, you will have real work to do there. It all begins here though, so listen to God's guidance on awakening:

And God Whispered…

"You shall radiate my light in the world. This is a message for your time. It is simple and clear and accessible to all conscious beings, as truth always is. Open, clear, and understandable by even the simplest of beings such as those who have not been educated by the world. My celestial realm needs to be available to all who wish to reside in it.

And I reside in every creature, in even the smallest particle of every object and being. For I made everything in the universe from light. Within each tiny atom, which is primarily space, I reside. This is how I come to know what has been created.

Yet humans have separated themselves from me and live in their ego which was designed by me to be a tool for living on the material plane. It was not meant to be an end in itself. Those who separate themselves from me and live in their ego cannot know me… they only can know about me, for the intellect only looks at things outside of itself and then creates names for what it observes.

The intellect is merely a tool, one that is separate from what it studies and observes. Intuition, however, becomes part of what it seeks to understand, and 'feels' the reality of what it embraces, rendering true understanding of the essence of all that it perceives.

Thus, to know me is to realize me within… to 'feel' my presence and to flow with the Spirit which is my energy of creative love. Now is the time to awaken to these truths and to emerge from the dream delusion of earthly life; to emerge from the boundaries of ego and to walk with one foot in the eternal realm of my abode; to flow with the river of liquid light created by the movement of my Spirit within all beings in my creation. Now is the time to awaken from the long sleep induced by the heavy vibrations of planet earth due to its position within the Galaxy. For hundreds of years planet earth has been entering a new vibration which is a finer vibration and brings the reality of a new consciousness to human beings on earth…to you. Open yourself to this vibration and drop the old heavy ways of thinking and dominating and controlling.

Emerge from the slavery of human designed groups, from the control of governments and organizations and become free. In that freedom, you shall form new communities of humans who work with each other to provide an earthly environment of true spirituality that will help form a new culture that will exist to assist humans in realizing their divine nature and assist them in expressing their inner soul talents.

Each human is directly connected to me and will find guidance and authority within that connection. There will be no need for governments or institutions in the new world that will be created. Eventually government, religion, education, and all means of production will be transformed into serving all of humanity, rather than dominating and suppressing as has been the case for many thousands of years.

In this new world culture, everyone will live in mutual love and cooperation, in joy and peace and all will reverence me within themselves, within all others and within all of creation. Their footsteps will be my footsteps disappearing on the sands of time yet remaining in the vibrations of earthly life.

All will become my instruments, my ministers to life and to others, blessing all others on the way with the light of Oneness. Now is the time to awaken to the totality of this truth; now is the time to enter the vibration of the new era of peace and love. An era I have spoken of through many of my sons and daughters of past ages.

Awake my child awake, and walk with my presence, awake, for this is the message for your time."

For Pondering

When you live in your ego and close yourself off from others, from the world, and from God, it is as if you own a huge mansion and choose to live in one small room; never venturing out to the more expansive areas of your home. Work on becoming aware of the totality of your 'being home' and learn to flow with the streams of light passing through you and within you so that you can get a grasp of your spiritual journey. Go deeply inside, beneath your mind and desires and 'feel' what is there for you.

If you live in this awareness of being and flow with your Spirit, you will be able to deal with any difficulties that cross your path and continue your journey towards complete freedom and awareness. It is time to tap the inner wisdom and strength that is available to you within your Self.

Contemplative Prayer

Father of Creation assist me in reaching and dwelling in my true inner Self so that I will be able to feel your guidance in each and every moment of my life. Help me to eliminate the distractions of the world as well as the tempting urges that desire to lead me astray. I am your child and as such desire to always have an awareness of my divine nature born from your touch and cultivated by your 'Whispers'.

Meditation

Allow yourself to enter within the space of your inner Being where the truth of your Self and the connection with All That Is exists. Breathe in and out slowly and deliberately until you feel a sense of your peace and inner joy. From this place, you have awareness that can expand into the far reaches of the Universe and into the true power of your Being. Feel, with your inner Self, all that is available to you as a Divine Child of the Universe. This is where God can 'Whisper' into your ear what you need to work on in your life. Allow that message to flow into you and just Be with it for as long as your Heart desires.

Affirmation

I am aware of the Truth of my Being which is One with the Divine Flow of the Universe. In this place within, I am joy, peace, and love.

"Dive deeply into the well of my consciousness"

CHAPTER 3

All that you need is within you. You do not have to search the world for secrets or hyper educate yourself, placing letters after your name. You have access to all truth and all spirituality through your connection with the Divine. Additionally, there are sources of truth passed on to us through scriptures and teachings that we may encounter. The important thing to keep in mind is that there is always an inner meaning to what is given to us, and we need to use our intuitive perceptions to properly understand what we find. The first principle is that whatever is encountered in these resources must resonate with our being. Without resonance there cannot be truth. Listen now to the 'Whispers" for further clarifications:

And God Whispered...

"Drink from the well of my consciousness, from the truth of my being which I have given to all creation. It contains layers of wisdom from the material level all the way to the still silent ambience of my pure consciousness.

Open yourself to all knowledge that lies within. Develop your Being so that you can understand what is available to you. This is the age of direct knowing. After a short period of time tuning in to my collective universal consciousness you will not need the limited, outmoded, and superficial learning that has prevailed on earth for hundreds of years. You will learn directly from within your own Being.

During other more advanced ages of the past going back many more centuries than you think possible, there existed a direct connection to the celestial spheres and a constant communication with Spirits. Humans had the ability to learn from the universal collective consciousness within the inner silence that I have always made available to beings on earth.

In that collective consciousness, you can learn of these advanced cultures that had access to knowledge as well as access to the free flow of energy available from the many suns. All suns are connected to each other and flow directly from me. Suns are my living children. Open yourself to your sun whose energy can be absorbed and stored and render your primitive energy sources outmoded. Open yourself to my Oneness collective consciousness during your special meditation times with me and while you walk in your daily activities be a receiving station… and you and your world will benefit greatly.

The more individual humans that drink from my well of consciousness, the more quickly life will evolve on the earth. The more human receivers of higher vibrations that exist, the greater the flow of universal knowledge into your planet.

Awaken to these possibilities now. Then you too can make spiritual progress on your journey. As you give to others from what you receive you will reap tenfold in knowledge and understanding. Put your ego aside and make yourself open to the field of consciousness that is available to everyone. No ego can receive the divine wisdom of collective consciousness. No ego may ascend to celestial heights. No ego or chattering restless mind can be charged with divine grace until it is able to tap the silence and peace within.

Learn the ways of the world teachers throughout the ages who have disseminated methods to enter the holy of holies within the heart of your consciousness. World teachers have known and taught my truth since the beginning of life on earth.

The key to inner realization of truth is accessing the deep inner feeling within your being and intuition which is the quickest means to drink from the divine fountain. Intuition is soul intelligence, far superior to any of your ordinary faculties. Venture into your inner heart and sit at the feet of those who have filled themselves with my love and wisdom. Open yourself to those who have become fully realized in me and you can then become my authentic ordained ministers on earth.

When you are fully conscious of what I have fostered in you, you will become ordained by the fire of my truth; ordained by the wisdom of eternal consciousness; ordained and blessed by the love of my heart…thus ordained, you will be able to bless others with the joy of Oneness.

Be with me; be in me; become filled by the source of all truth, in this way, you will also avert the organizational karma that plagues every religion shortly after its founder leaves. When one of my world teachers leaves the earth, his/her followers, who are on a lower level, attempt to interpret the divine teaching of their teacher who drank from my well of wisdom. Still not free of ego, however, they desire to take control and dominate while feeling that they are carrying out the mission of their teacher. Thus, a dilution and distortion of the truth that was left to the world begins to set the teacher's mission in a different direction contaminated with the desire to control and dominate.

Take comfort, for I never control or dominate my children. I want them to discover me within themselves by their own will. Still, the clarity of a teacher's mission remains available beneath the distortions.

Available in the well of my truth where you can drink deeply of the original essence of every religion and spiritual movement, no matter how badly it has been distorted.

In truth, all religions and true spiritual movements are one in me in their essence. All are designed to bring you home to me and to awaken you to the truth of your being and to help you to open yourself to the well of pure consciousness that flows from my being directly to your essence.

At this time, I am placing a call on all human hearts to awaken, for now is the time to enter into my Oneness. The new spiritual age is upon us."

For Pondering

Education has stifled spiritual progress on the planet. Through immersing the consciousness of those being educated in mental gymnastics, memorization, and ego expansion it has produced generations of people who are convinced that 'they know'. When one feels he or she knows, one is closed off to new knowledge. Further when a new proposition reveals itself, it is immediately crushed because it doesn't fit the knowledge of a given field.

For example, there have been many discoveries about the pyramids in the Giza plateau that suggest that they are much, much older than has been taught by Egyptology. Because these new revelations do not fit the standard beliefs of the Egyptology that is being taught, they are rejected out of hand. Truth always makes its way through however, so eventually teachings will be adjusted to accommodate the new findings. It thus takes much longer for knowledge to expand. Basically, when one studies a field of knowledge, one studies an old history of the field that will be adjusted in his lifetime.

Direct knowing with intuition will change this old pattern as more and more people drink from the well of universal consciousness.

Contemplative Prayer

All beings of light and spiritual friends help me to forge a powerful connection to the celestial realms in which you live and work. Help me to begin my spiritual work while I'm here, ordained by the truth that is given to me from within. I wish to become a minister of Oneness and Truth in my life, always ready to assist others on their spiritual path. Accompany me, strengthen me, guide me as I proceed on my journey on earth and after I leave. I bless you and accept you as my spiritual tutors and sources of wisdom and light. Help me to radiate love and light to all persons that I encounter.

Meditation

Follow your breathing until you reach a quiet state within. Visualize yourself as a Being of light that can travel throughout the

Universe and observe any reality you wish by merely thinking of it. Feel the existence of energy passing from many suns in our galaxy into our sun and then into the earth. This energy feeds the earth and all conscious beings that live on it. Not only can you absorb this energy, but you can ride on it and allow it to carry you from solar system to solar system until you reach the Central Sun of the Universe from which this energy emanates. Feel the warmth and gentle loving power of the Central Sun. Allow yourself to merge with it and feel Oneness with the entire Universe. Sit with that realization for as long as you like and then gently allow yourself to return to your normal consciousness.

Affirmation

I am a Divine Being made of Light and Energy. At the root of my Self I live in Oneness with All That Is in the Universe. I radiate the love and joy of Oneness to all I encounter on my journey through life. Through Oneness, I am ordained as a minister of Truth in the world.

"Believe in me, not the world"

CHAPTER 4

What do you believe and how do you conduct your life? Do you lean heavily on the external knowledge you have loaded into your brain network? Do you identify with your earned degrees and letters after your name? The knowledge we identify with as ours is often the thoughts and creations of other humans, which involve theories, intellectual fantasies, and distortions of reality. Wouldn't you rather drink from the well of wisdom that is available from the Creator of the Universe? Wouldn't it be much better to soak in the truth rather than the distorted fantasies of others? Let's listen to what God 'Whispers' about what can be accessed from within your own being:

And God Whispered...
"If you believe in the world and in what it has taught you, you do not believe in me. If you compare what I am telling you to what your mind has been programmed with, you lose the truth of my 'Whispers'. For only in being open to the possibility that I am teaching you something entirely new and revolutionary compared to commonly held ideas, will you have the possibility of living a life in concert with me.

Hold these truths within you as themes for a new world and you will benefit by their life-giving energy. They will seep into your consciousness and help you to learn how to dive further into the well of wisdom within.

Do not accept anything without testing it in the resonance of your being and consciousness. If you feel you must reject what I am saying…then do so, for even if you are not ready to embrace my truth you are still my child. One day you will recognize your kinship to me and seek to open your connection with me.

I will never dominate or manipulate you or any of my creatures. The scriptures that speak of an angry revengeful God are distortions. They are projections of human frailties onto me of the desire to dominate and control. I am love and gentleness, joy, and wisdom. I invite; never compel.

Just these last few lines will cause many who believe in the distorted scriptures to reject what I am saying. That is acceptable through the principle of free will, yet one day they too will realize the truth, perhaps in this life, if not, then most certainly in the future

Everyone will eventually make their way back to me…I have seen it, since for me time does not exist. For those who are ready to hear me, then let us proceed. Let us walk down the path to freedom and enlightened consciousness together and come to full realization of the truth.

If you are ready, let us proceed to create an awakened world, a new garden of innocence, blossoming with life in me, a garden full of flowers with the aroma of truth that fills the air.

At this time, the truth that does exist on earth is mixed in a porridge of untruth and agenda filled thought. As a child, in innocence, you open your heart, but as a grown conditioned adult, you are closed. Most of what you think is filled with self-interest and the desire to dominate…the product of the dominance-oriented world.

Learn to be as a child, innocent and open and free, never worrying about whether you will win or lose, nor concerned with tomorrow or yesterday…but only living in the moment of now, because life on your world and all worlds is a continuous series of now moments. Keep your consciousness in the present and drop all your agendas if you are to progress spiritually. Be with me and in me, within the deepest part of yourself. Walk with me into eternity"

For Pondering

Imagine a world of openness, love and innocence; with people living to express kindness and assistance to others. The purpose of such a world would be to live, love and learn about the truth of existence and to build a society where everyone is happy and able to express their most cherished inner desires. Now consider what our world is like with dominance, distortion, expressions of superiority and elitism. It is clear that we need to work toward creating the spiritual world of openness and kindness described above.

We can accomplish this by going inside of ourselves and drinking from the well of truth and then expressing our inner realization in the world. Over time and through other realized aware beings, the world will change. It will become a world of Divine Children playing at reality and bringing joy to others thus raising the vibrations of the planet and the Universe.

Contemplative Prayer

Source of all goodness and light, I open my mind and heart to your wonderful promptings. Help me to discern truth from worldly delusions so that I may be a light for others on my earthly journey and afterwards in the heavenly realms. Bless my walk with your 'Whispers'.

Meditation

Enter your inner quiet space and visualize a world of light joy and peace in which you are floating in the air as a ball of light and energy. Everywhere you go you are radiating goodness and love and you are changing the world into one of peace and harmony by your presence. Feel what that world would be like and continue to love it into existence. Feel yourself as an instrument of positive change.

Affirmation

I will express the light, love and peace in my daily walk through life. I am an instrument of the Divine and as such I am obliged to lift up everyone I encounter and assist in raising the vibrations of the planet.

"This is your call"

CHAPTER 5

The fact that you are reading this book likely means that you are being called to a high vibratory life. Answering this call will create a new and powerful life of grace and goodness for you and those around you as you radiate the Oneness vibration to everyone in your life circle. Open your inner feeling to what is being given to you in this chapter. Understand the calling so that you may choose to answer it. The 'Whispers' are for you:

And God Whispered...

"This is your call to answer that which has been vibrating within you before you were born and that is calling on you to walk away from a consciousness limited by your body and your world. Calling on you to drop all attachments that have bound you, attachments to planetary life, to the external, to identification with the transitory, to lower vibrations.

It is enough, now you must venture beyond the limits of your ego cage that holds your perspective to the earth, to limitation, to a small existence. Remember, you are my child. You are vast, you are a consciousness filled with the power of my creation, you are divine…walk with me now in your divinity.

You are a royal personage, feel your dignity, feel your benevolence, feel your own power of being, your ability to love, to bless, to empower.

Leave behind your small selfish actions and depart from your egotism. Drop all concerns, all agendas. Be honest, straightforward, and even-minded; be loving, caring and gentle, be master of all you survey. Do not think that all of this is beyond you, for are you not my child. This is your call to awaken; your call to Be in me and of me, your call to recognize your true nature.

Venture down the path towards eternity and leave behind the path of death and despair, confusion, fear, and doubt, suffering and sadness. Can you hear this call?

It is your time for freedom. The call is but the first step into eternity. You will need to work on expanding your consciousness into my being and into my omnipresence, for I am the ultimate teacher, master and guru with whom all teachers have blended in order to pass on my light.

But now I come to you directly because many of you are ready and can move forward with my help and guidance. You will be led to situations and teachers that will offer further assistance. And if you are sincere and persistent, the goal shall be yours and you shall walk with me through earthly life and into eternity. You shall realize your Oneness with me."

For Pondering

The time to awaken has come. Consider that you have been asleep for many, many years in your lifetime. From what need you awaken? Awaken from identification with life. Awaken from what has been programmed into you through your earthly 'education'. Awaken from the hundreds and perhaps thousands of put-downs inflicted upon you from others. Awaken from the many false ideas you have about yourself and from the limitations you have imposed upon yourself. Awaken from the dictates of dominant life-crushers that have crossed your path. Awaken from all that is false within you.

Only the truth about your nature can change all of this, along with higher vibrational energy within you that proceeds from the source of the Universe. Ponder and feel all of this and allow yourself to embrace the possibilities that abound in your life! Awaken to freedom, to joy and to truth so that you may begin to ascend on your path toward eternity. Deeply ponder what this means to your inner growth and expression in life and beyond.

Contemplative Prayer

Beloved God and Angelic Helpers assist me in awakening from the sleep of life on earth that keeps me in darkness and limitation. I desire to awaken to the light and wisdom that is available through Oneness in you and to those who have achieved an awakening from all that the earth teaches. Bless my path with your awakened love and light. Help me to answer the call to Oneness.

Meditation

Go inside quietly following your breath (*focus on your breath until your chattering mind calms down and you become quiet*) until you feel a shift in your consciousness that floods you with peace and joy. You are a Divine Being that is connected to other Higher Beings of Light; connected to Great Masters that have overcome their earthbound consciousness and live in dimensions in the Universe beyond the material. You are connected to Angels and angelic helpers ready to assist you. You are connected to God, the

Oneness of All. Feel all of that and know that you are special; you are unique; you are Divine; you are free. Feel your divinity and rest within it for some time in the knowledge that you will become Oneness realized in this lifetime.

Affirmation

(Repeat Affirmations aloud first, then more and more quietly, then as a whisper, then silently within.)

I am a Divine Being with attributes of divinity that will be realized as I grow into my true nature. I am connected to and have help from highly realized Beings that are working to raise the vibrations of the planet and the Universe.

"Where you go when you die"

CHAPTER 6

People often wonder about where they will go when they die. In scripture they read about heaven and hell, but the accounts are quite sketchy regarding what occurs on the other side of the veil. Death remains largely a mystery. God certainly knows what happens there and gives us critical aspects of the afterlife in the 'Whispers' of this chapter. We are also given many pointers as to how to better prepare ourselves for our life in eternity. Listen now to what God 'Whispers' in our ear regarding the afterlife:

And God Whispered...

"There are many mansions with many rooms in my abode in the heavens...each holding a specific vibration. While on earth, there are mixed vibrations, in the afterlife, vibration determines where a soul goes and what other souls gather around it.

Your soul signature is comprised of the vibrations you leave earthly life with. These vibrations, be they coarse or fine, will ultimately take you to areas of similar vibrations in the heavens. After an initial greeting upon arriving in the heavens that is filled with unconditional love and acceptance, you will be provided with spiritual emissaries that will lead you to where you belong.

What you do not realize in your earthly consciousness is that your vibrations on earth are leading you into situations that will resonate with your vibrational nature. As you continue to act on what you are attracted to because of your vibrational tone, your signature becomes stronger and stronger.

On the other hand, it is possible to change your vibrations on earth through prayer and meditation practices as well as the avoidance of negativity and self-destructive habits. This is worthwhile spiritual work because it is very difficult to change your vibrations after you leave the earth.

There is no gender in the afterlife, though Beings may choose to appear as male or female. Souls choose a gender when they enter earth. While one gender predominates; both female and male energy exists in all beings. On many planets, there are beings without a separate gender who hold both male and female energies within themselves and can procreate through the pure use of their own will.

Humans once had this ability but have lost it as they became more and more immersed in physical matter and identified with one gender or another.

Death is merely a transition to another vibratory level and exists on all vibratory levels except when beings reach full Oneness with my being. Then they are free to merge with me or exist in a unified but individual state according to their will to carry out my universal work of progressive growth and learning that continually works towards completion.

Individual Being expressions make this process rich in diversity and allows for limitless expressions of beauty and joy. Only those who have ascended above material living can appreciate this richness and beauty. So... open yourself to the beauty of new expression when death approaches, do not fear but rather simply allow and follow, for my love extends to you wherever you exist.

How many beings appear to their loved ones after passing over to tell them how beautiful it is where they are and that they should not worry but know that they are still in existence and doing fine. If more humans would break free from their matter consciousness and open themselves to Spirit, they would not fear death and then life would flow much more beautifully on earth and humans would be happier.

They would grow spiritually and not waste so much time on nonsense, drama, and delusion. Embrace the beauty of death so that you may live more completely while in physical form. Know that you are more than your physical form to make possible the ascension to higher levels of vibration that are necessary to awaken to my presence within you, while you are on earth. It is much more difficult to awaken after you leave.

If you are conscious or awakened at the point of death and you have worked towards awakening and living in my presence in your life, but have not reached full awakening, you will be allowed to continue your work in the afterlife.

If, however, you have not seen the need to work at awakening and die in an unconscious state, your vibrational level will determine where you reside in the afterlife and your work there will be determined by other considerations in alignment with my universal laws.

Live in your Spirit, live in my presence, and you will be guided to awakening. Follow your Spirit into complete awareness of me…into awareness of your true state as a child of God.

You are made of God-stuff… pure energy… pure light…pure consciousness… pure bliss. We are One in each other, know that and live in it now. Awaken to the truth of your being and live in your 'I Am' consciousness and you will rise to Oneness while on earth and live in Oneness throughout eternity."

For Pondering

When you ascend in your consciousness you will not fear death. You will realize within yourself that death is merely a transition to a different dimension or realm. When you die in an un-awakened state you will automatically go to the place that holds the vibrations that you leave the earth with. If you have lived a low life and have harmed people on your path, you will go to a lower vibratory place, and you may have to endure suffering there.

If you have lived a good life and have been kind and helpful to others, you will go to a place of good vibrations and reap rewards. Bad is bad and good is good, but neither are awakened. If you die having awakened, you will go to a place of learning where you will learn what you need to do to further your journey to full Oneness realization. If you transition fully awakened, you may go to another level entirely and continue your growth and learning there. You will be given useful work to do helping others there and/or on earth. The work of the Universe is ongoing and all pervasive. It will be a joy to be a part of it. You can begin that work here in your life on earth. As you awaken to Spirit you will be guided as to how to begin assisting others in their ascension to Oneness.

Contemplative Prayer

Beloved God, Oneness Spirit of the Universe, assist me in my journey toward living within your Spirit and radiating love and light to all those that I meet in my life. I love you and wish only to be within you and live in your presence. Be with me God. I will begin my eternal work while here and look forward to serving you in Oneness throughout eternity. Amen.

Meditation

Enter your quiet place within. Chant Om mentally at your Heart Chakra in the center of your chest. Feel the sound of Om vibrate throughout your being. Know that it is the primordial sound of the Universe. Stay with Om...Om...Om continually. Know that you are stepping into the afterlife when you go inside; the more you feel this the more it will be possible for you to leave life in an awakened state.

Affirmation

I am an eternal being of pure Spirit whether I am in the body or in the afterlife. I will work at complete Oneness realization until I am in a permanent awakened state and can go to the next spiritual dimension after leaving the earth.

"You are the only you that you are"

CHAPTER 7

Uniqueness is a quality that many people desire to have. This is especially true since the way of life on earth can be very robotic. People are creatures of habit and often their habits own them. Underneath their habitual robotic nature however, humans are unique and have an essence of specialness that transcends their habits. More importantly, the ability to grow spiritually and overcome mechanical habits is an integral part of the inner nature of human beings. We are each unique as designed by our Creator. Let us tune in to what God would like us to know:

And God Whispered...

"You are the only you that you are, and you came into existence by my finger of love. I wanted to extend my consciousness to all levels of my creation so that I could 'feel' the reality of every corner of the universe.

I created many kinds of conscious beings to occupy my worlds in addition to other beings lacking a divine conscious nature and I maintain a constant direct connection with each of them.

What is very important to know is that I provided each conscious being with a way out; a way back to me. I gifted them with divine consciousness and the ability to activate it on their own. Thus a few have found the way back to me through their own divine nature and they left roadmaps to help others do the same.

There is only one way back to me, only one way of truth, but there are differing expressions of that way depending on the one who established it on earth.

During each age there are special challenges. Every time the world seems to completely lose sight of me and of truth, I send an ascended being to create a fresh and new way home to me…a new expression of spirituality, a new path. Though it accomplishes the same result; a way back to me, it has other elements relevant to the age it came and embodies inclinations of the teacher who left the path.

Within each conscious being there is a key to liberation from the delusion of sleep, which is the lack of inner awareness in which most humans live on earth. This key tugs on them throughout their life until they acknowledge and accept it. Once acknowledged, it can be worked on to free one from the entrapment of material life. After life on earth all will be further clarified in special centers of learning on higher realms.

You have come into this lifetime with many impulses as part of your Being that need to be accepted and acknowledged as real and a part of you. These impulses are a part of your uniqueness. Some need to be worked through; some need to be understood; others need to be discarded. This is your spiritual work and will finally become integrated in your own unique awareness.

These impulses are a portion of your karma, so that thoughts you have had and actions you have taken even within your imagination and desires have become imbedded within you. Some you have brought from your existence in the celestial realms before birth while others have been formed during your lifetime on earth.

Accept these as part of your nature and allow yourself to discover everything that exists within you. Proceed on your journey of inner discovery, then you will be able to find your way back to me.

Don't judge, just accept, you have judged yourself many times and have paid the price of harm you have done. But now you must awaken and place your consciousness totally within my Oneness. Then, your negative impulse seeds of karma will be burned up and disappear from your nature, provided that you do not give them energy, but instead, give me your energy and love.

Then you shall find your way back home to my heart where I have prepared a place for you."

For Pondering

Why do most people become so caught up in the world and unable to make spiritual progress in their lives. One main reason is identification. Through identification people worship aspects of the world rather than God and higher energies. People become what they identify with on earth; money, power, education, cars, houses, clothing, body enhancement, wealth, poverty, food, the list is endless.

In identification we put our personal psychic energy into things or into roles and experiences in life, thus losing the ability to use that energy to ascend and transform ourselves in Oneness. Desires drive identification, so we need to become aware of our desires and of the ways in which we identify.

The best antidote to identification, however, is to go inside and experience our inner landscapes and to feel connected to Oneness. This will eventually dissolve our outer identifications and assist us in ascending in our Being to higher levels so that when we leave the earth, we can continue our progress of spiritual growth or, if permanently in Oneness, we will be able to move on to higher realities.

Contemplative Prayer

O God assist me in settling into my divine nature which is connected to you and the universe. Help me to know that I am not my habits and identifications with the world but rather the pure divine essence with which you endowed me as one of your children. My deepest desire is to realize my Oneness with you and all of creation.

Meditation

Sit cross-legged on the floor or on a cushion or in a straight chair with your feet on the floor keeping your spine straight in either position. Go within and feel your Being at your Heart Center. Follow your breathing by breathing in to a count of 4 or 6 (whatever you can do easily without straining) and breathe out to the same count. Do not stop in between but breathe in and out smoothly and evenly while also keeping your focus on the Heart Center. When you are centered within begin to chant Om internally at the energy centers of the Heart, then at the point between your eyebrows, then at the top of your head. *(Focus your awareness at these energy centers as you do this exercise)* Keep repeating that sequence: Heart, between the eyebrows and top of the head in that order (do not go backwards). This meditation helps you raise your energy up through these three chakra energy centers on your spine. Continue this technique until you are feeling peaceful inside and for as long as you like.

Affirmation

I am light, energy and Spirit. I seek to connect with the energy of the Universe so that I will become one with All That Is and dissolve the identification with the world and all earthly desire traps. I live in Oneness.

"My universe is constantly recreated through change"

CHAPTER 8

Habitual robotic nature hates change. Change takes us out of habit and forces us to be spontaneous. It pushes us to be creative. Habit only works with known patterns, so when a change presents itself, habit seeks to crush it in order to retain its robotic ways.

Change is a powerful tool for spiritual growth. Change enables us to become more aware of what is occurring in life. It forces us to become internally oriented and weakens our identifications with the external. Listen to what God tells us about change and your personal unique soul expression:

And God Whispered...

Embrace change, for through change you will arise out of darkness and into the light. Do not retreat from change because it is the unknown for the known will keep you in prison within your comfort zone, but through discomfort new ways of being will arise in your Being.

So... forge on ahead and embrace the unknown and needed change will appear in your life. I gave you the will to make your way back to me; to break through your temperamental blocks and to create ever new realities within yourself. I gave you the consciousness to become a co-creator of the universe with me. Then, use your will judicially but without restraint, always respecting and empowering others on your way.

Often, to achieve what they desire, many of my children trample over others, creating new obstacles for themselves in negative karma. Use your will to break new ground but always be sensitive to the spiritual needs of others while at the same time not letting anyone hold you back. For those in darkness do not want others to achieve the light, whereas those of the light desire everyone to share in the light.

Gently, but firmly, claim your will to positive change and growth. Go deeply within and bring forth your individual soul expression for just as I have placed the desire to return to me within your Self, so I have also endowed you with special gifts, talents, and expressions.

You will not attain me until you bring forth your deepest soul expressions, for in these lie the keys to unlock your universal consciousness. Expressing your soul's nature will also help others in your life to feel themselves in a new way. Soul expression is a key element to spiritual growth, one that is overlooked by many teachers.

This is the reason why great athletes, great musicians, great singers, great artists, great humans of any expression, move others profoundly causing them to feel a bit of their own divine nature and provoking the divine impulse to Be, to come home to me.

The way to energize your true soul expression is to drop the impulse of safety and security that obstructs the internal energy seeking expression from deep within you. Each person has a deep soul desire to express; to create new form and new culture. So, don't feel that you are the exception and lack this inner drive for you have but to discover your unique soul quality.

Look to your childhood before you were conditioned by parents, peers, and earthly education; look to your essential qualities. Your essence sought expression before it became dulled and beaten down by adults.

This is the way of delusion...those imprisoned by delusion crush the Spirit of the young to ensure the continuance of the delusional cage. Aware, creative, consciousness is very threatening to the world and for this reason it has been very difficult to maintain the purity and force of true spiritual movements. As soon as a spiritual leader leaves the earth, a process to break down and distort the teaching begins. Most followers of realized beings are limited in their understanding of truth and they begin to make 'improvements' which are actually... 'distortions'. These 'improvements' turn into dogmas and institutional regulations which further confuse truths and principles taught by the realized being who was steeped in my universal Oneness consciousness.

The institution built up around Jesus is a prime example of such distortions. Many early forms that grew up around the teaching of Jesus were declared heresies by those who rose to worldly power early in the movement even though many of these 'heresies' were actual teachings of Jesus based on Truth.

Some of the most ingrained in delusional consciousness became hailed as the leaders of the movement, and throughout the past two thousand years, many distortions have reined over the truth that Jesus taught.

Yet, because of the power and light in the Being of Jesus, many have come to me in alignment with the institution built in his name in spite of the distortions.

The same process of distortion has taken place in every major religious movement on the earth…no exceptions. Consider those who advocate killing others in my name. I would not urge anyone to kill except in defense of one's life. Any religious leader who has advocated killing or torturing other human beings has acted from the depths of darkness, totally apart from my Oneness.

Please know that the sincere desire to realize me within yourself will always receive a response. Your way out of delusion can take many forms and you may find support from many true movements that have been established on earth. The most important change you can seek in your life is a search for the truth of your Being which causes you to seek me within your life. Embrace this change for I await your return to me and do not delay your journey home to Oneness in me. Follow the divine urge within you to change and transform yourself into the divine child that you are in essence. This change is one that urges you to peel off the layers of untruth that cloud your true essence and transforms you into the beacon of light that you are as my child."

For Pondering

The Universe abhors passivity and lukewarm ways of being. There is a fire in the belly of everyone reading these words and if you haven't enacted your passion fire, read the chapter again for ways to find your true soul expression which seeks to explode from you into the world.

About 25 years ago I was living a rather ordinary life in many ways, but something kept gnawing at me to join a church choir and begin singing. I had sung and played guitar earlier in life but had moved away from music to focus on business. Well, I finally heeded the urge to sing and was led to a church and joined the choir. Shortly thereafter the parish decided to use song leaders to lead the congregation in song. I became one of four new song leaders in the parish...I was hooked!

My fire exploded within me and before I knew what happened I was leading song in 5 different parishes on a weekend rotating schedule. Since then music has become my soul expression; singing, playing guitar, writing songs, and leading singing groups with contemporary songs. It has changed my life because I now have a powerful soul expression that lifts my Being to great heights.

Powerful soul expressions lie deeply within all of us. If you have not already done so, find yours and begin its expression.

****

A word about the commentary in this chapter about how powerful spiritual messages get diluted after a great one, such as Jesus, leaves the earth. In the fourth century, a rather worldly and political leader named Constantine used his power to select what books would remain in the Christian Scriptures and which would be removed. He then saw to it that what was kept was edited severely removing much of the spiritual content that could lead people to their own realization of God within themselves. Next, he overlaid the legal structure of the Roman Empire over the Christian Church and rendered it a political power in the world until it began to be challenged during the Reformation in the 16th Century.

Though churches offer an environment that can assist in bringing one closer to God, the real work must be done by the individual person on his or her own. That is the essence of this book...to offer a teaching for everyone, religious and non-religious alike.

Contemplative Prayer

Beloved Lord Jesus lead me to the complete truth of your original teaching for I desire to draw ever closer to you and to our Heavenly Father. Help me to keep your presence within my heart so that our two hearts join as one. I love you and seek to be your divine brother now and forever. Amen

Meditation

Begin by using the same technique as in the last chapter:

Sit cross-legged on the floor or on a cushion or in a straight chair with your feet on the floor keeping your spine straight in either position. Go within and feel your Being at your Heart Center. Follow your breathing by breathing in to a count of 4 or 6 (whatever you can do easily without strain) and breathe out to the same count. Do not stop in between but breathe in and out smoothly and evenly while also keeping your focus on the Heart Center.

When you are settled in peace add this mantra technique. Stop counting and allow your breath to flow naturally. As you inhale, mentally chant 'I am' and as you exhale mentally chant 'One with All'. Inhaling: 'I am' exhaling: 'One with All'. If thoughts invade your process focus again on your mantra. Continue as long as you are feeling calm and peaceful keeping also a focus on your Heart center. Fifteen minutes to a half hour is a good starting place.

Affirmation

I am peace. I am bliss. I am consciousness. I am a child of the Universe. I will express my unique soul expression in life. I will discover my inner fire.

"Open yourself to my ordination"

CHAPTER 9

This chapter is your special invitation to play a role in changing the world profoundly. It is about receiving the spontaneous blessing of an ordination, not by any religion or spiritual group, but directly by God, the Oneness of the Universe. You may continue to walk through life as in the past but with a personal blessing that will enable you to be God's minister in life, a source of blessing to others. This will not be through what you say or what your intellect contains but rather through what you radiate externally to others from the source of all goodness through your soul and spirit. Open your mind and heart to God's words:

And God Whispered...

"Take these words within your heart and become ordained as my minister on earth. Many religions and organizations have lost their way as they are more concerned with the salvation of their institutions than in guiding humans to freedom of Spirit and to Oneness.

They are administered mostly by those who live in their ego, how then could they lead others to awakening? Therefore, I am ordaining those of you who open yourself to my truths and to my universal consciousness within your being, those of you who are pure in heart and desirous of assisting others in their awakening.

Merely by living in Oneness, and radiating my love to all those you encounter, wherever they are in their spiritual growth, you shall go forward as my direct ministers who will bless others, teach them by example and lead them home to me.

You do not need earthly education nor letters after your name to be my minister, simply my direct connection within your Being. You will only need to access that connection which is available to each of you.

Those of you that open your hearts as well as your minds will receive my many gifts that touch the most hardened heart. Those sincerely and regularly seek my presence within will carry that presence to others.

Those who are my ministers of Oneness are imbued with my consciousness and live in their Spirit rather than in their ego. The following signs indicate the attributes of my ordained ones who live in a working relationship with me:

- Ø a constant desire for the truth
- Ø an ongoing desire to live in my presence
- Ø a sincere desire to lead others to me
- Ø an inner quietness that pervades their consciousness
- Ø an ability to think, feel and act without restlessness
- Ø a cultivated daily practice of entering the silence
- Ø a ready feeling of devotion towards my Spirit
- Ø a spontaneous awareness of the existence of a divine nature in everyone

- an ability to feel my universal Oneness consciousness within and around themselves
- a strongly developed intuition
- some indication of the ability to prophesize
- a natural feeling and desire for righteous living
- an ability to discriminate between what is spiritually depleting and that which is spiritually enhancing
- a deep desire for equality among all humans
- the ability to receive truth from me directly
- the reception of special gifts of the Spirit
- a deep desire to create a world that empowers and instills spirituality in all humans

All of this and much more can be yours if you but open yourself to my presence within you. Be my minister and instrument on earth and your journey home will be faster and smoother. You don't have to <u>do</u> anything, merely to <u>BE</u>, to BE within my Oneness and radiate it to others. For as you help others, you shall be lifted up, as you love others, so shall you be loved.

This is the way of my universe, become a minister in my field of Oneness. This is my invitation; the choice is yours."

For Pondering

What does it mean to be ordained? Usually, it implies a connection to a religious organization and requires years of study in scripture and/or religious practices, counseling, and other training. The main ingredient is an inner calling to lead others to God or assist them in their spiritual evolution. The rest is fluff and may be unnecessary unless the prospective minister is a complete novice. Intellectual training may actually cut one off from her or his inner flow and fill one's head and ego with a lot of 'knowledge'. Everything you need is within yourself. Once you have a strong inner connection to 'Oneness' within, you can assist others to do the same.

At a certain point within your evolution God may 'whisper' to you in the silence…*'You are ordained as one of my ministers in the world'* or you may simply 'feel' the ordination within you and you can proceed to bless others and gently guide them in their lives, with their permission, of course. Often you can help in conversations about their life issues without ever disclosing anything about being ordained. In fact, it's better not to mention your ordination at all, just do what you are called on to do without any credit or accolades… simply be a good friend.

When I say permission, I mean that whoever you are connecting with will bring up their issue and seek your input…it's that simple. Listen first, really listen and then talk with them from your heart which knows much better than your mind. Bring together your heart and mind and 'feel' intuitively the state and issue of your friend that is seeking advice from you. Speak from your heart and from the truth and let it sit with him or her.

People often go to multiple friends and relatives for such advice, so don't be disappointed if your friend takes wrong advice from someone with a worldly or cliché mentality. Simply, gently and firmly state your truth as you are intuiting it. Remember 'intuition' is the intelligence of the soul, far more powerful and reliable than intellect. When you receive a strong indication that you are ordained by God or the Universe as a Minister of Truth and Light; take your Being forward into the world. Until that time you can practice ministering simply by being a kind and good friend to others.

Contemplative Prayer

O God, you are my life, my joy, my peace. Teach me to love as you love. Teach me to always be in you. For you are everything I need and desire in life. You are God my savior, my light, my love. Help me to radiate you to everyone I meet.

Meditation

Take a quiet walk in a park or somewhere in nature. Be sure to leave your phone in the car. No interruptions allowed. Clear all thoughts of your life and issues. Focus on where you are in this 'now' moment. Feel the energy of the Universe all around you; in the trees, in the wind, in the birds singing to God, in the animals rushing about in the brush, in the warm sunlight, in the floating white clouds making skyscapes, in the gentle babbling brook… even in the rocks and soil. Now feel that energy beating your heart, flowing into your breath and powering your body to walk along. Now sit on a bench or rock or anywhere and collect all these feelings without naming them; just feel the energy. Sit for as long as you like in peace and joy.

Affirmation

I am a child of the Universe. I flow with the cosmic energy that enlivens me and powers my consciousness. I am endowed with a spiritual energy system that allows me to evolve spiritually. I am One with all that exists around me in nature and in the Universe.

"You can come to me in many ways"

CHAPTER 10

In this chapter God reveals many secrets of the spiritual malaise in the world and how religions have failed in the task to promote the awakening of consciousness on the planet. There are reasons why humanity remains asleep in their identification with the world and why those who are powerful in their sleep state are attempting to take over and control all humans on earth. They will not succeed because God is now calling all humans to enter within the power placed in their own consciousness. Listen carefully to what God is sharing and deeply feel the content of God's 'Whispers':

And God Whispered…

"You can come to me in many ways, depending on your level of consciousness and your individual inner needs and inclinations. I have always provided, through my special ones, the means to contact me and find your way back to me. Even during the darkest ages of material consciousness, such as the one from which you are emerging.

In the East, I have continued to provide the direct route of meditation and contemplation for aspirants, but I am now offering new means to raise your inner vibrations and make spiritual progress much more rapidly, thus helping to raise earthly consciousness into a completely new vibration. Everything on the earth will be changed because of this change in consciousness. Let us now focus on the new possibilities that exist.

When my son Jesus came, it was during a truly dark and heavy vibration, called the material age in the West and the Kali Yuga in the East. During this age, there was little love and understanding and little ability to rise above the most mundane of earthly concerns. brutality and all kinds of unkindness were the primary ways of life on the earth. At that time, little love, little understanding, and little awareness was experienced or expressed.

The male gender with its physically stronger nature completely dominated. While love did exist in the hearts of many women, it often could not find expression except in relationships to spouses and to children. But it was quickly subjugated by the coarse and heartless behaviors that dominated life then.

In this atmosphere, Jesus brought my love to the world and the message that everyone is a child of mine, a child that has the capacity to be One with me as Jesus was. Yet Jesus could not teach the inner ways to reach me in meditation in the same way as the East, so outwardly focused was the consciousness of that time.

Instead, Jesus taught his followers how to reach me in prayer and contemplation. To his closest disciples he provided access to the Holy Spirit which they were able to transmit to others and use for healing. His mission was primarily to the West which I designated as the arena of conquering the material world. He also spread my powerful teaching of love in the East which was the keeper of Spiritual principles and techniques for becoming One with me. The West would work on making progress in living conditions and technologies that would serve human life on earth.

But now the time has come for the East and West to bring together what they have learned for the past two thousand years. The East will adopt the technology of the West and apply it in unique ways and the West will become open to inner spirituality in the midst of technological living.

Spirituality will thus differ in the way it is implemented in the West and material progress will take new forms as it is applied in the East. The world will then merge into a unified life of spiritual growth assisted by advanced technologies.

Forms designed and evolved from the teachings of Jesus led people to me through prayer, song, and ritual practice. People gathered first within homes and secret sites that later became churches. In monasteries and convents, a more inner spirituality was practiced allowing religious monks and nuns to go deeply within themselves to connect with their soul and Spirit.

Since Jesus there have been many who have attained a closeness to me because they filled their consciousness with thoughts and prayers to Jesus. This made it possible for them to transcend their material nature and come to me.

I will always leave a path for those that sincerely desire to come home to Oneness in me, yet most have remained outside of that possibility in the West and now, many of the monasteries and convents have disappeared.

Institutional churches hold little interest in providing a way to raise the consciousness of their members. Other spiritual developments have created new opportunities for growth as more and more sincere devotees seek direct communion with me through meditation, contemplative prayer, and other practices that I am guiding the world to provide.

Inner awareness and direct communion with me will be the norm and many will enter Oneness with me and attain advanced states of consciousness which will create a new conscious vibration that will affect the consciousness of all human beings on earth.

In this way, life on earth will be completely transformed into one of peace, love, and harmony. Poverty, disease, and war will be eradicated and spiritual aspiration towards Oneness will be supported and fostered everywhere, helping to create a spiritual harbor for aspirants on planet Earth.

Seeking ideal conditions for their growth and spiritual unfoldment, earth will also become a playhouse for spiritual expressions of every kind. Music, dance, art, architecture, and other expressions of Spirit will reign supreme as a most esteemed way of living.

Education will radically change moving from mere memory training to creative enhancement and the development of individual soul expressions where the person's desires for expression and growth will determine educational needs and the style of learning required.

Teachers will cease to be needed and will be replaced by learning facilitators who will gently guide students on their journey of development. Information will be accessible through technology similar to today's computers but will be much more advanced and be capable of interacting with the thoughts and questions of developing learners.

Higher education as it exists today will cease to exist and be replaced by specialty schools that will help learners to focus on their specific area of interest. All education will be free of charge.

Society will provide everything needed...food, shelter, energy, and transportation for free in turn for service to society by its members who will receive small stipends thereby creating a living circle of positive creative manifestation and progress.

Many will practice both internal spirituality through meditation and external spirituality through outer forms of devotion and contemplative prayer while some churches will continue to exist for those preferring structure or ritual, as a tool to enhance the inner growth of members. Ritual can be a powerful tool for inner growth and should continue to be offered in churches.

All forms will be acceptable as long as people sincerely desire a particular practice but for those who simply attend services because they feel that they must and yet do not make themselves present to my Spirit, no such accommodations will be able to continue. Such superficiality is profoundly meaningless.

The new era will not be a time for superficial organizations or churches. One day everyone will awaken to the real possibilities within themselves and those with any sincere desire to find me will be rewarded for I have said many times through many of my chosen ones, 'Seek and You Shall Find.'

At this time I have sent new teachers to provide the means to reach me directly without having to go through intermediaries of any kind. People will be taught techniques for energizing their Spiritual beings that will enable them to reach me directly and those who succeed in reaching my consciousness within themselves will be ordained directly and internally by me who will then offer help and assistance to others in ways and methods as to how to reach me.

Since the old Eastern model of the guru is no longer necessary for Spiritual progress, meditation and prayer helpers will be available to assist new aspirants.

Teachers and guides can help aspirants from any realm in which they exist and work. All will flow from my being as humans realize on a massive scale their own divine natures. All of my special ones, known and unknown, will be available to assist the new arising consciousness on earth.

A new spiritual culture will arise which will be brought into manifestation through the creative power that I have bestowed upon my human children."

For Pondering

In order for the transition to the new world that is sketched in this chapter a new form of association of communities must evolve. In such a world, government is not necessary and is counterproductive spiritually. No idealistic 'isms' such as Socialism, Communism or even Capitalism should be proffered to the people by any government. Government will fall by its own weight of suppression of freedom. Let's be clear; all efforts to impose new ideologies on the people of the earth will fail, causing much suffering. Government needs to fall away with its taxes and laws and corruption. The world of politics is a horrible reality and brings out the worst in those that live in the political environment. Money also needs to disappear with its greed and power and terrible magnetism. Those who worship money cannot enter Oneness. Money really does not exist; it is merely a means of exchange.

Be advised that nothing has to be done about these issues... burn that into your consciousness...nothing has to be done, directly, about these issues. Everything will come about naturally as the world embraces spirituality and evolves into a spiritual environment. The only thing you can and should do is to go inside and work on your own Oneness connection!

Contemplative Prayer

(Chant this prayer to yourself three times then close your eyes and feel the power of God within you) Be still and know I am God. Be still and know I am God. Silence opens the doorway of your heart, be still and know I am God. Your heart is mine says the Lord, your heart is mine says the Lord, live in your Spirit and I will come to you, your heart is mine says the Lord. Seek the kingdom of God, seek the kingdom of God, and all else will be added, seek the kingdom of God. The kingdom of God is within, the kingdom of God is within, all around you and inside you, the kingdom of God is within. Enter the kingdom of God, enter the kingdom of God, within your heart we are One, enter the kingdom of God.

Meditation

Go inside following your breath to a count of 4 or 6. Evenly and smoothly in and out. Continue until you are feeling calm and peaceful. Cease the counting and start your mantra "I am' as you inhale and 'One with All' as you exhale. "I am…(and)…One with All" continue and go deeper and deeper, dwelling in your inner calmness. You can vary this technique by chanting internally "I am Peace" or "I am Joy, or "I am Love", or "I am a Divine Child of the Universe". You could also do these in a series starting with "I am One with All", then "I am Peace", chanting all five mantras slowly and continuously. Always go back to the first mantra ("One with All") to restart the series of mantras.

Many spiritual aspirants practice this or similar techniques for hours and hours. No pressure though; practice as long as you feel comfortable. Even fifteen minutes daily will bring great results and profound changes.

(You can also chant these mantras eyes open internally while you drive, cut the grass, or do other chores or while walking in nature.)

Affirmation

I am reversing the flow of my breath energy and sending it up my spine daily and in so doing I am weakening the hold my senses have on me and opening myself to Oneness.

"Follow the flow of your Spirit"

CHAPTER 11

How can we follow our internal path to God? What special triggers has God placed within us that will lead us forward in growing spiritually and departing from delusion to awakened consciousness? In this chapter, God reveals both the reminding tugs and the process of guidance that is available to us as his children. God also provides seven specific guidelines for us to follow in order to keep ourselves on the right path to awakening to Oneness. These 'Whispers' are both instructive and clarifying, let us listen:

And God Whispered...

"Follow the flow of your Spirit for I have set the pathway back home to me within you. There is nothing that is not available to you from within the depths of your Being.

No educational or religious institution can provide what you already have within, and I have arranged it that early in life you begin to receive little tugs on your consciousness which you experience as feelings and inspirations and often as a guiding inner voice, a still inner voice that can draw you home through the maze of delusion.

Some heed these tugs while others are so distracted by chaotic world energies that they are not able to feel the tugs. Many bury them beneath the force of their karmic desires where they merely fade away. *(Karmic desires are generated by our thoughts and actions in life, especially towards others)*

Since the world does not have knowledge of the tugs, it urges humans not to pay attention to them or discredits them as useless emotions, However, those that take them seriously and follow the guidance received from their Spirit are led to what they need in order to grow spiritually.

Some have books that they are ready for, virtually jump off shelves into their hands and others witness common occurrences in life through a prism that offers them new meaning or clarification. They then are moved to ponder deep questions as a result that will lead them to the inescapable conclusions that life is much more than humans make of it... much more than the world teaches, that there are lessons and a mission that they need to carry out.

That there is a constant natural flow of energy back to me, the stream of which may be entered by any sincere seeker. These lead to the lessons of the Spirit within.

So, follow those tugs, hunches and inspirations and see where they lead, be aware however, that your Spirit will never lead you into trouble or into behavior that will hold you back. Thus, you will need your discernment to sort out the value of what you are being urged to do or think or feel because you will also be tugged by your karma as well as by negative energies that seek to keep you entrapped in delusion.

I have given you discernment which will help you to feel the difference between a tug of your Spirit and a distortion of reality by your ego or karma, or the worldly conditioning of your personality.

You will have the intuition to measure what you are receiving against the normally understood behaviors that I have endorsed through the ages as guidance.

Here is guidance that may offer you parameters to follow:

1) Honor your commitments in all ways until you have received an indication that you need to move on…then find an honorable way to conclude what you had begun.
2) Do not deceive others or speak untruths.
3) Honor your parents, elders, and inner teachers.
4) Do not steal energy from others or take something that is not yours.
5) Honor the Spirit in everyone since everyone is one of my children.
6) Do not hurt or harm another human being in any way except in defense of your life.
7) Stay true to your inner Spirit.

These basic guidelines will help you discern your path, otherwise, your expression in life has a very wide range and you may make any contribution to life on the earth that you feel is worthy and beneficial, leaving your mark.

Go into your inner well of universal consciousness at least once daily; twice daily, morning and evening is even better, offer prayer and meditate seeking Oneness. This will help you bypass the restlessness of your ordinary mind and will open the inner pathway of your Spirit to your consciousness.

Ponder the truth that has been brought forward in the great scriptures and writings that you have been drawn to. Love all others and don't hesitate to help them, when given the opportunity.

Ask me for assistance on your journey and do not hesitate to ask for anything that you need for I will give you what you need, not always what you want.

Follow the glowing energy I have placed within you, and you will arrive home in my universal Oneness consciousness."

For Pondering

Learn to read with your consciousness, rather than your intellect.

(Technique for Conscious reading: Sit in a meditation posture with your spine straight and follow your breathing for a few minutes so that you are feeling calm and peaceful. Hold the book open at your heart level and begin to read, feeling as though you are pouring the contents of the book into your Being. 'Feel' what you are reading and know that it will become a part of you.)

When you read with your Being and your consciousness you absorb what you need permanently. Reading this way allows you to read a truth bearing teaching over and over again without becoming bored or feeling saturated. Every time you re-read the book or scripture you will absorb more of what you need until you own the teaching within you.

While reading in this way don't analyze, memorize or associate with other readings. To do that is to be intellectual as taught in typical earthly education. It will give you only a superficial knowledge of what you read. But you will not own it. You may be able to speak 'about' it, but, again, you won't own it.

When you speak 'about' something you are separate from it; it is not a part of you. When you own it, it's as if you wrote it yourself. Remember, no analysis, no comparisons, no associations. Being intellectual closes you off from Spirit and is harmful to your spiritual unfoldment. Unfortunately, though, it is the way of today's world.

Being intellectual is a closed loop. You know what you know and no more… you are not open to new knowing. Openness leads to spiritual growth and development. This book is written for your Being and to lead you to spiritual growth. It is written to your consciousness, not to your mind. Therefore, read it with your consciousness and with your Being.

Contemplative Prayer

Beloved God and Angelic Helpers remind me often of my divine destiny of living within your all-encompassing Oneness presence that exists everywhere in the Universe. Guide my steps to the full realization of my eternal spirituality. I am a child of Light and Love.

Meditation

Another walking meditation: Take a walk in a park or in the woods. Start off by breathing in to 4 and out to 4, smoothly, evenly. This could be challenging for some because you are splitting your awareness between walking and breathing. Continue until it feels like it's flowing nicely then stop counting and allow your breathing to continue on its own. Feel as though there is a shaft of energy coming down to earth and into the top of your head…into your crown chakra and down through all of your chakras filling you with divine energy. Walk this way for about five minutes and then sit on a rock or bench and allow yourself to feel bathed in this energy. Sit as long as you like and when you want to stop say mentally 'finish' and allow the energy to level off and your normal waking state to return. This is a powerful technique so don't try to jump right back into daily activity too quickly. The longer you feel the energy the better it is for your conscious development.

Affirmation

I am a child of the Light and maintain a constant energy connection with the Universe. I can cause my energy to vibrate within me as often as I like so that I feel the reality of my Spirit.

"This is how my universe works"

CHAPTER 12

What is the design of the Universe and how do suns, planets and moons relate to each other? Is there a flow of energy from the center of the Universe throughout galaxies and solar systems? You can discover a new understanding of cosmology from what God shares in the 'Whispers' of this chapter. Prepare yourself to be astonished:

And God Whispered...

"This is how my universe works... From the well of my consciousness, I will explain just how the universe is designed. Your science has discovered only a small portion of the planetary systems I have designed.

There are many material planets or worlds arranged in solar systems and found within galactic systems, which you have already discovered.

What you have not seen, however, is that just as I have maintained a connective thread with you, I have also spun a flow or channel of energy reaching into all galaxies and suns within them. Suns maintain a connection with each other constantly exchanging energy so that each receives energy from other suns and transmits energy forward to planets which transmit energy to their moons. Each sun, planet and moon are progressing in individual evolution just as you are evolving in consciousness.

Nothing in the universe is in isolation or stagnation, everything is in some process of change. Space which appears empty is charged with subtle ethereal energy which connects your material energy to the next dimension of existence.

There are seven dimensional levels emanating from the realm of my existence which is also known as the Central Sun, from which every kind and level of energy flows. Everything flows from me outward and ultimately works its way back to me.

I have created many, many forms of beings and worlds for them to live on and grow. They thrive on other planets, moons and even suns, living in a form relevant to the world on which they exist.

Those that live on suns, for instance, exist in their energy form, constantly being charged with the interactive energy vibrations of their sun world. For this reason, there are so many that revere and worship the sun on your planet. They are remembering their highly charged sun world existence and desire to feel, even at a distance, that loving warm sun energy.

Suns are divine beings unto themselves which carry out their planetary roles in the Universe as I have ordered them from the beginning of time. Now is the time to open yourselves to these realities and grow beyond your earth-bound limited consciousness.

Many of you cannot relate to earthly life and may have great difficulty with the ego-driven, self-centered human manifestations that dominate earth cultures. Yet, as your planet aligns with the galactic center and your sun transmutes these lower conscious energies into higher vibrations, earthly life will begin to reflect higher vibrations and more spiritually based cultures will arise out of the old domineering ways of living.

This has already begun as your planet and solar system transition into alignment with your galactic center. This progression through the ages or Yugas has been taught in your ancient civilizations which have described various levels of energy existence from the dense to the very fine.

These ages are relative to your solar system's position within the galactic system and the relationship of your sun to other suns. Each age affords different energies and different opportunities for spiritual growth.

Thus, there are many worlds, many life forms, many kinds and levels of consciousness operating in the universe. Moving now back to your world, you can enter your inner life which will confirm with the awareness that has been implanted within your consciousness and cellular DNA.

Know this; I maintain a constant connection with all Beings, planets Suns and will never leave you alone or isolated. Open yourselves to these truths and my love for you which is the essence of my connection with all of existence.

Your earth is about to explode into a new way of living. Open yourself to all possibilities, open yourself to the finer vibrations which are about to create a new signature of my grace, energy, and love on earth."

For Pondering

Living in ego is living within walls of separateness. It is you against the world. Everything and everyone exists outside of you and are different than you; sometimes inferior, sometimes superior. The ego is a closed loop and whatever we do think or feel within ego does absolutely nothing for our growth and evolution. How can we get out of the ego loop?

We can extricate ourselves from the ego cage by going inside and opening up to the power of Oneness. Begin slowly by simply quieting and calming restless thoughts through techniques provided in this book which come from ancient practices in the East. As we learn to go deeper and ultimately learn how-to live-in Oneness permanently, we, little by little, free ourselves from the bondage of ego. Ego means being closed to possibilities. Oneness means being open to the Universal flow of Divine energy.

That is why Jesus said, "Except ye be as a little child ye cannot enter the kingdom of heaven." Little children are wide open to growth and have not yet formed ego. The kingdom of heaven is the inner realm of Oneness. Jesus taught the disciples how to enter Oneness and that we are each a child of God. His message was formed into a closed loop by the those who claim to teach what he taught and by changing and editing the writings left by his close followers. Another example is: "The kingdom of God is within." which Jesus said. It has been translated out of every version of the Bible except the King James.

Whether you are talking about individual or organizational ego; it's the same story. The loop needs to be kept open building and maintaining a relationship with the power of Oneness. Once a certain number of individuals are living in Oneness; once organizations begin to promote, and support Oneness; the world will become a the spiritual environment it was meant to be.

Contemplative Prayer

Divine Oneness help me to understand everything I need to know to evolve spiritually into one of your ministers on earth. I do not seek to gather mind stuff from schools or from others but rather to dive deeply within my own consciousness that is directly connected to you and the Universe. Amen

Meditation

This is an eye-open meditation that you can use while driving, walking, cutting the grass, doing chores around the house or any situation where you don't have to interact with others. First, shut off all radios, CD's, TV, computers and turn your phone off. You will not want to go deeply inside and change your state as in regular meditation.

With this technique you are training yourself to keep both your internal state and your ordinary consciousness working together in your awareness. Begin chanting a string of mantras internally; I am Spirit, I am Peace; I am Love, I am Energy, I am One. Go back to the first one and repeat the sequence of mantras, feeling the reality of each one while you do. Do this as often as you wish and as long as you like. It is very refreshing and soothing.

This technique could also be used as a prelude to a regular meditation session for fifteen or twenty minutes and then sit for a deep internal journey with one of your favorite meditations in this book. Better to occupy your mind with mantras than with worldly chatter.

Affirmation

I open myself to the Oneness of the Universe every day as often as possible in sitting meditation, walking meditation and while doing chores in eye-open meditation. I ponder often, seeking to feel truth within my Being.

"This is what keeps you from me"

CHAPTER 13

What are the obstructions to spiritual growth? How do we prevent ourselves from understanding the truth of our Being? In this chapter God will pose 27 Questions for you to ask yourself that will lead you to discovering all you need to know about what may be blocking your way to Oneness. God does not desire to preach or give sermons, but rather to offer effective means to create change that will lead to a spiritualized planet for beings to learn and grow into Oneness. And now the 'Whispers':

And God Whispered...
"This is what keeps you from me... those of you that can hear will understand how you have been separated from me, you who are lost behind the veil of blindness that keeps humanity in the dark will be unable to understand what I am saying.

You have but to open your inner heart and inner awareness to receive this most essential truth. It is not a simple matter for that which binds you is intertwined with every aspect of your ordinary consciousness and is embedded in your cellular structure; in your ordinary mind and emotions, in how you see yourself and perceive every aspect of everyday life.

When I unveil the truth every cell in your body, and every particle of your ordinary consciousness will rise to define and dissect this truth. It will rename it; marginalize it; discredit it or make you feel that it is something you know and understand already.

For this reason, I will unveil this truth without naming or describing it, instead I will lead you from afar with a series of questions that you can ask yourself and then you can formulate for yourself the truth of your sleeping consciousness.

So, let us begin...

> Question 1: Do you feel restlessness or a discontentment that you cannot seem to resolve?
> Question 2: Are you constantly seeking to be praised and recognized by others?
> Question 3: Who do you think you are?
> Question 4: What do you think you are?
> Question 5: Do you feel as though your thoughts are distant from you and not connected to your feelings? ...or are your thoughts centered within your Being?
> Question 6: Do you feel that you can control everything and everyone and that you can shape what they believe about you?
> Question 7: Do you feel that you have no control over anything?... that your impulses have complete control within you?
> Question 8: Are you ruled by reactions to everything around you?

Question 9: Are you closed to new learning, or do you feel you already know?

Question 10: Are you open to new ideas about reality?

Question 11: Do you feel a connection with the universe?

Question 12: Do you pray? If so, what do you ask for? Are your requests always centered on what you want or need?

Question 13: How have your prayers been answered?

Question 14: What is it that you want most from life?

Question 15: Do you understand why you are here?

Question 16: Does 'being centered' mean anything to you?

Question 17: Do you say what you mean and mean what you say or are your words empty of meaning?

Question 18: Are you truthful all; most; some; or none of the time?

Question 19: Are you honest with yourself or do you do those little mind twists that always make you right?

Question 20: Can you spend quiet time with yourself, or do you always need to be doing something?

Question 21: What is it that drives you in your life?

Question 22: Do you need the opinions of others to decide what is true?

Question 23: Or do you understand that the answer lies within you?

Question 24: Do you always get lost in the details of life and miss the truth?

Question 25: Do you feel that everyone is different but that there is an underlying sameness in all humans?

Question 26: Do you feel separated from me?
Question 27: What is the one truth from which everything else flows?

Ponder these questions, one at a time, for a time and you will arrive at what is real within you, the one essential truth of all of existence in the universe. Take as long as you like and keep pondering these questions, one at a time, until you have, without a doubt, reached the Oneness of your being, the essential core Self that is within you; that essence that you have carried throughout the ages, then you will no longer need to ask; there will be no more questioning…no more doubt.

Reflect on a question without seeking a quick answer, that is to ponder until the answer arises from within you. There will be complete certainty when that occurs and you will understand the answer within the depths of your being, then in that truth, you and I will be One."

For Pondering

Why do we leave our earthly body? There are many reasons for leaving the physical body. Some leave because they decided to leave at a certain point when they entered this life. Others leave because of reasons that lead them into a juncture with certain events that cause death. Some individuals have a death wish that is granted. Yet others are called to leave because they finished what they needed to do in this life. Some people become so closed in on themselves and closed off from divine energy that they simply wither and die, often leading very deadened existences for a long time before they leave the earth.

Those that find ways to connect with their inner relationship with God or the Universe; with their Oneness can extend their time in this life. That is because the connection with Oneness offers new opportunities for spiritual and personal growth and evolution beyond what they had set out to accomplish in life. With Divine energy, the goal post can be moved out and new possibilities can be created. This is one of the reasons for this teaching to be given at this time. Many individuals are near reaching new possibilities in their lives and they can find encouragement and teaching within this book. It is time for many humans to cross the threshold into a new way of living that is in concert with the universal flow of Divine energy.

Contemplative Prayer

Beloved God assist me in discovering how I am obstructing my way to you. Help me to know how to change my ways so that I may flow freely into your Oneness and Universal Divinity. I am your child. Teach me your ways O Lord. Amen.

Meditation

Pondering is thinking while meditating. You can deepen your pondering as a meditation. Go for a walk in your favorite place, in a park or in the forest or sit by a gently running creek. Before you begin this pondering/meditation, read one of the chapters or For Pondering sections in this book, one that has especially touched your heart.

Then let your thoughts and feelings flow freely as you ponder the message of the chapter. Ponder (don't analyze) why you are moved by the content, see if you can feel the connection to something within you that has stirred your heart. Listen for 'Whispers' to your Being. Ponder for as long as you like and throughout the day after you leave your nature sanctuary. What important life lesson seems to call from within your chosen reading? What message lies within the reading specifically for you?

Affirmation

I am a dynamic Being with higher spiritual faculties. I can reach anywhere in the cosmos with my consciousness. I am a child of the Universe.

"Live In your Being"

CHAPTER 14

What does it mean to be a Human Being? What is the difference between intellect and intuition? Why are people so superficial in their relationship to life? Why are people doing, doing, doing constantly? What is the real Self and how can we tap its power and energy? These are the key questions addressed in this chapter as God unveils the essence of being human and the how we can truly understand our relationship to the Universe. Tune in to these 'Whispers' and learn how to BE:

And God Whispered...

"Live in Your Being, you cannot find me if you are constantly doing, doing, doing, and running around day and night with all kinds of activity. You cannot find peace in the midst of frenzy.

You will never find joy in restlessness. Life is action, it's true, but you need to learn a new kind of action, a quiet action that is internal. You can call this action... Being. You can learn to Be.

In Being you can contact your real Self, which is part of your Being. It is in that Self that I sent you on your journey to find me. It is in that Self that you can find my presence hiding in the silence. It is in that Self that you can commune with me and feel my vibration.

When you learn to Be in your Self; then you can really act in the world and your action will have real power and create new waves of vibrations on the earth because what you do will have my imprint on it. Your action will cease to become restless and superficial. It will become powerful and meaningful and carry my love out into the world. What you do will have soul-power, the soul power within your Self; within your Being. Your Soul-Self-Being action will have a profound effect on the flow of life on the earth and will lead more souls to me and my love.

Before you learn to Be, you cannot truly understand, you only delude yourself that you "know". Understanding requires my truth coupled with your Being. Thus, my wisdom that exists within your Self. To truly understand requires intuition.

To develop intuition, you need to go into the silence, and swim beneath the restless churning sea of your personality/ego which you have formed in response to your world, your environment. In the silence you can touch and experience your essence. With intuition, you can know anything you wish to know by merely tuning into it.

With your intuition, understanding and inner silence connection, you can fulfill your destiny as co-creators of the Universe with me.

There are many pitfalls in the delusion of ordinary life woven for you to work through. Intellect is the chief tool that will keep you locked in the web of delusion. Some have used their intellect to reach me, but it is a long, tedious, and difficult way.

Without intuition, the intellect is like an empty tin can, drowning out harmonious melodies with loud harsh noise, deafening and obscuring the truth with thousands of echoes of untruths, comparing... associating... dissecting... complicating.

Abstract knowledge will keep you trapped in the dream of delusion, because intellectual knowledge is under the 'Babel Principle' in which truth is mixed with untruth. The 'Babel Principle' makes it nearly impossible to discriminate Truth from untruth.

If you but live in your Being, in your true Self, and use the intuition therein, truth will make itself clear to you thus you will see through the 'Babel Principle'. You will understand...you will become a knower.

Real understanding is when truth blends with your Being. Intuition is the bonding energy that makes this possible. In your quiet, peaceful Being...you understand and can 'feel' the truth within your Being-Intuition-Energy. Truth comes from me, and truth will set you free from the bonds of ignorance and delusion. As you go into your silence, you will find me; you will find my truth.

In restlessness, you will be controlled by your karmic actions, and in restlessness, there is no clarity. Restlessness perpetuates further restlessness and keeps you from me, until you discover the silence within your Being where I can speak directly to you.

Only in me is your soul at rest. Be Still and know that I Am. Go into the cave of silence...Feel your Self... Feel your Being...There you will find peace...There you will find Truth...There you will find my Spirit...And you will be able to flow on a river of light that leads to my Oneness. Live in your Being and BE One with me, then your journey will end in me, in my Oneness."

For Pondering

People on the earth live primarily in their minds, in their bodies or in their emotions. Mind, body or emotional consciousness, though normal, is a limited way of living. Such consciousness will not bring about spiritual growth. Living in Being and Spirit assisted by awareness creates higher energy and will result in increased evolution and ultimately lead to Oneness. To live this way permanently, it is necessary to explore inner dimensions and consciousness. Eventually one achieves Oneness expanded consciousness even while conducting ordinary life. No one would be able to detect this from the outside but the one living this way knows the difference and is able to see through the many drama-based agendas operating in others. Learn to live in your Being in this way.

Contemplative Prayer

Lead me to the way of living in my Being and my Spirit so that I can always be aware of you within me O God. Even while I am living my ordinary life, remain in my awareness with your presence. Then it will be possible to leave this life as your minister and servant and permanently enter your eternal Oneness.

Pondering Meditation

Quiet down and follow your breathing until you feel the silence that is within you. Dive deeply into that silence beneath the restlessness and frenzy of life. You can feel the contentment of your inner sanctuary always available to you within yourself.

Feel your Being. Resonate with it. Learn to live in your Being no matter what is going on in your outer life. This is the quiet action you can perform constantly. Learn to BE. You are a human Being, not a human doing.

Your True Self lies within your Being in which you came into this life. In your True Self, you can feel your connection with God and all of Creation as One. Your Being actions will create new waves of vibrations that will cause positive change in the world. What you do will have true Soul Power. Thus, your Soul-Self-

Being action will profoundly affect the flow of life on earth leading many souls to seek Oneness in God. In this way you will become a Co-Creator of the Universe. Sit with these thoughts and feelings and allow yourself to integrate this pondering meditation within your Being. Let us design mantras for this meditation.

> My True Self is within my Being
> In my True Self I can feel my connection with God and Creation
> My Being actions in the world will create positive change
> My Being action has true Soul Power
> My Soul-Self-Being action will profoundly affect the flow of life on earth
> This action will lead many souls to seek Oneness in God
> Soul-Self-Being action will make me a Co-Creator of the Universe

Chant these mantras internally in order over and over for this Pondering Meditation.

Affirmation

I am an Eternal Being; One with All That Is. I am a vibration of the Divine Force of the Universe. I will work daily to reach the Divine Eternal Being within myself and allow it to expand into my life. I am a Co-Creator of the Universe…

"Choose the energy that will lead you to me"

CHAPTER 15

Constant choices present themselves to you daily. Will you choose to adopt actions of lower, coarse energy or those of higher, fine energy. One set of choices leads to a deep immersion in the world while the other will lead to living spiritually. One is the way of kindness and love while the other is the way of dominance and control. One is the way of peace while the other eventually leads to conflict and war. The lower path is one of separation while the higher path is of togetherness under God. The impact of these choices on the world will be profound. Listen to these 'Whispers' carefully...

And God Whispered...

"Choose the energy that will lead you to me, choices will unfold before you constantly, choices to head in the direction of good or of evil, choices to build a world of kindness and love rather than one of greed and despair; to lift up your brothers and sisters rather than to outdo and dominate them; to exalt yourself or to humble yourself before others; to crave things, money and power or to seek the treasures of the Spirit. These choices present themselves constantly until you eventually flow towards me and eternal conscious life, or towards the world that will enclose you within the chains of your actions until one day you decide to choose freedom in me.

The choice of worldly living, for power, lust, greed and egotism is imprisonment in the way of error and spiritual ignorance while choosing the higher path, of living in goodness and light bring joy and contentment, has its difficulties and challenges.

Most people have chosen the other way and often look upon those of the light as inferior and weak, criticizing them among their brethren and conspiring against them.

Once you have chosen therefore, you need to find like-minded individuals with whom to befriend and spend time. Your intuition will guide you to them and you will know each other when you meet. You can discern by vibration those you enjoy being around and you will be astounded by the similarities you share with them, even though you may not agree on everything, you feel very comfortable and deep contentment in their company. You will simply enjoy their soul content and feel an inner magnetism toward them.

Small groups of such people are beginning to form throughout the earth as the energy of the planet becomes more conducive to building a spiritual world. This is the time that I have predicted would come and is the early stage of a new era for humanity.

It is critical that everyone strive to make a choice for freedom and spiritual living. I have called many of you to make this choice and to reject the old ways of dominance and power. Choose love, brotherhood, peace, and harmony to establish the foundation of a new spiritual environment on earth.

As a critical number of you choose the way of spirituality and freedom, many more will be able to feel the vibration of the correct choice in their awareness. Thus, the world will be transformed, and a Golden Age will arise. Poverty and hunger will no longer exist because an enlightened humanity will not allow others to suffer.

While those who live in greed have much more than they need yet continue to want more; justice exists whenever everyone is concerned for his brother and sister and loves their neighbor as themselves, ready to empower and encourage growth and ascendance in them as the need arises.

A spiritual world exists when everyone feels others as a part of themselves and separateness ceases to be the operant tendency in human consciousness. This is how Oneness enters the consciousness and is the new theme for human existence on earth as well as throughout the universe.

What does the energy feel like that will lead you to me? You will feel lightness and joy whenever you open yourself to my energy invitation. As you allow my energy to enter your Being, you will drop all resistance naturally and experience a healing and soothing flow of grace that will lead you to people and events that will help you to grow and express your special unique gifts and talents. You will know the feel of it deep within your being as a familiar energy that seems part of your Being...as familiar as your own breath. You are rediscovering what has been a part of you since you were born into Oneness eons ago, the Oneness brought into this life with you.

Since you are open to these 'Whispers' from me you are open to the inner truth that you hold within your

Being. A truth that you will awaken to as you proceed in Oneness energy. There are obstructions and traps that you need to have awareness of so that you can progress in your spiritual life.

Here are the traps of worldly energies that can impede your progress:

➤ Seeking Money and Material Gain

You will notice that when you give yourself over to the energy flow of seeking money that you feel 'driven' by thoughts and feelings of building your personal empire. You seem to become obsessed by seeking material energy of many kinds and forms and it is difficult or impossible for you to stop your thoughts and meditate on me or enter the silence or hear the universal sound of OM. You are thus driven away from me, but you have before you an option, a choice for change that you can activate throughout your life on earth...a choice to live in light and peace and create loving kindness in your life circle of family and friends.

➤ Seeking Lust

When you give yourself over to lust you become absorbed in the energy of pleasure and sexual thoughts and your body, mind and emotions become driven by the desire for sexual expression. Sexual expression without love will drive you away from me more quickly than most other human activities. You will find that if you make this choice for lust, it becomes impossible for you to quiet down within yourself. You will be like an engine that is always idling fast wasting energy, driven by your thoughts and feelings of sex.

It is also repugnant for you to go quietly within for lust robs your being of finer energies that are necessary for the inner quiet of meditation. Yet you can still turn yourself around and choose to move away from lust and place your mind on beneficial spiritual reading of scriptures and other writings of those who have chosen a spiritual way of life… and to listen to and benefit from my 'Whispers'.

> Seeking Power and the Expression of Egotism

When you seek power over others and its accompanying egotism and self-inflation you become unreachable because you think that you are me. Yet at any moment your life could be taken from you, or your life could be altered by accident or illness. Make no mistake…I do not make these things happen, but your karma in this life can dictate a sudden change at any moment.

The deeper you immerse yourself in a power journey, the more you call to yourself and your family accidents and tragedies. How often do you hear about these things occurring in the lives of those who have accumulated power? The further you go into power and egotism, the blinder you become. The energy of such a journey feels like a movie of yourself in which you are playing a role in which the desire for others to give you adoration is nearly unstoppable. Those that dislike you are relegated to the realm of the ignorant and stupid because you feel that you are right about everything, that you know everything. You feel omnipotent and indestructible, but of course, you are not.

Fortunately, everyone in power is not this way, for many have chosen to help others and have good intentions for their brothers and sisters that have often been given power as a result, otherwise the world would be in total chaos.

The battle of choices for good or evil exists on many levels, and when you are caught up in the blind energy of power and egotism, you are impervious to the subtle energies of spiritual growth. If you meditate while on a journey of power, you will find yourself projecting thoughts of achieving greater and greater power rather than settling into your finer spiritual vibrations.

Many people who have chosen power are in places of authority in the various religions of earth, so, in my name they acquire power over others and speak as if they have been guided by me. Fortunately, there are many sincere seekers of the truth in these religions or these organizations would be totally useless and harmful.

On earth, there is everywhere a mixture of truth and untruth, but that is all beginning to change as more and more humans choose the spiritual journey seeking to commune with me daily and seeking the energy of Oneness with me, with all other beings, and with the universe.

Sit with your spine straight and breathe evenly internally chanting 'I Am' when you inhale and 'Spirit' when you exhale. Do this until you reach the energy of silence, then sit in that silence for as long as you can. If thoughts begin to invade, go back to breathing with 'I Am Spirit' once again until you are quiet. Feel the energy there; dwell in it. Do this every morning and evening for at least half an hour.

Be with me in silence, And the changes you will see in your life will be miraculous. You will become quieter, more stable, and much more effective at everything you do. Most importantly you will be on the path to freedom. You will be my instrument on earth; ordained to bring peace and love to all others in your sphere of activity. Be your own minister and my minister by choosing the energy of inner silence and spiritual living. You can do this in the midst of your ordinary activities and responsibilities. Simply take the time daily to enter the silent spiritual realm within yourself. Remember me once, on the hour, every hour, feeling my presence within you.

Be at peace. Be kind to others. Do something for someone every day. Do these things and you will achieve Oneness in me and my Universe!"

For Pondering

To ponder is to reflect on a question without seeking a quick answer. Ponder until the answer arises from within you. Pondering is meditating on realty with your consciousness, heart, mind... with your whole Being.

Pondering Exercise: Take one question from each of the following and ponder it by asking your inner self to provide you with the answer. Keep mentally asking yourself the question over and over; gently and smoothly without forcing. If you receive an answer, fine, if not, at some point in the future an answer will come to you, probably when you least expect it. You can do this pondering while doing a sitting meditation; after using the breathing preparation; while walking, while going about your daily activities. The question becomes a mantra for you. Take one question a day for a week. The questions are from Chapter 13: I have changed the questions into the first person.

> *Question 9:* Am I closed to new learning, or do I feel I already know?
>
> *Question 10:* Am I open to new ideas about reality?
>
> *Question 15:* Do I understand why I'm here?
>
> *Question 20:* Can I spend quiet time with myself or do I always need to be doing something?
>
> *Question 23:* Do I understand that the answer to all questions lies within me?
>
> *Question 26:* Do I feel separated from God or the Universe?
>
> *Question 27:* What is the one truth from which everything else flows?

After the week, go back and re-do any question that really seemed to move you. Revisit Chapter 13 and take other questions that seems to call you and spend some time pondering them. This is the work of consciousness.

Contemplative Prayer

In you O Lord I find my peace. In you O Lord I find my love. Let me dwell within your Light, I define my soul in you. Listen to my call and answer me O Lord. Be with me in every moment for I am your child. *(You can use this as a mantra repeating it over and over. It will take you deeply within)*

Meditation

On a clear starry night find a quiet place on your deck or outside on a blanket in the grass, on a chaise lounge or anti-gravity chair so that you can lie back and look up into the heavens. Feel as though you are one with the stars above and that you are swimming in the night sky as a lake. Allow yourself to completely let go of worldly concerns and daily consciousness. 'Feel' within the depths of yourself that you are ONE with all that you see and that the stars are caressing you with their energy. 'Feel' the stars; 'feel' the Universe; 'Know' that you are One with all that is before you. Enjoy this experience as long as you like and then return to your ordinary daily consciousness in the knowledge that you just took a step closer to Oneness.

Affirmation

I am a Celestial Being and have come to earth from the heavens. When I peer into the stellar landscape, I feel my Oneness with all of Creation.

*"When you believe you know...
that's all you know"*

CHAPTER 16

Is your consciousness open or closed to new knowledge? If you feel you already know…nothing new can enter in. You are a closed book. How many people are like this? They aren't necessarily knowledgeable, but their attitude is one of superiority and closed mindedness. Such an attitude prevents even God from giving them a thought or inspiration. 'Be as a little child' as Jesus recommended, because children are open and pliable and are able to take in radically different thoughts and flow with them. Thus, the objective is to be open to new ideas and even radically different ways of looking at life. This, of course, is what this book is about… the 'Whispers' of God to our consciousness so that we can override our earthly conditioning. Embrace these 'Whispers':

And God Whispered…
"When you believe you know…that's all you know. This is the key to a new understanding on the earth. When you can understand this principle and employ it in all your thinking, The world will begin to change dramatically.

The principle is this… 'Never accept the idea that you know', That is; do not allow yourself the delusion that you 'know', Not who you are, nor what the world is nor how another person is nor a what a factual reality is that you have observed.

Everything...I repeat...everything that you take as a bit of knowledge, or fact of reality, has within it a deviation or exception from what appears to be true. An obvious example is the belief that the earth is flat that was held as common truth centuries ago, then humans discovered the exception to that rule and observed that the earth was round. Once people believed that the sun revolved around the earth...and that belief was also debunked.

Example after example demonstrate that solidly held beliefs were adjusted with new revelations and information. Yet, people would kill other people, and did so, in defense of false beliefs. So, when you believe that you know, you close yourself off from learning something new, from permitting reality to reveal itself.

Here is the key; keep to the following axiom of life:

"At this time, it appears that... 'a fact or observation or belief is...' yet I will remain open to new insights or revelations that may alter what I have learned. I will not close what I know and believe but will keep my consciousness open to new possibilities."

This is a way to always and in everything, retain an openness to fresh revelations, and a total reversal of what you previously believed is allowed to take place, if necessary.

Open consciousness is what is meant by 'being as a little child.' Children are so open to learning that they completely live in the moment. Adults can learn to remain open and live moment to moment too thus always having a fresh approach to every event and experience, instead of constantly dealing with new events from a previous belief, perspective, or experience. To deal with a present event with a previous conclusion is to live in sleep and close yourself off from new experiences. To deal with a current experience from what 'you know' is the same thing... sleep. Awaken to a fresh approach to each new day, each new hour, each new moment. Be open to others in a way that is fresh and new, as if you know nothing about them and you will see new dimensions in the people around you constantly. You will find friendship in those you thought were against you, you will find love in those you thought coarse and unfeeling, you will find compassion in those you thought harsh, and you will also see established patterns in the behaviors and thoughts of others, except now, you will allow for deviations in their expressions of themselves in life.

Be open to new dimensions in everything and everyone and life will completely change for you and for the planet. This is a critically important lesson in all that I am sharing with you. Go forth as a child of the light...in openness, in love, in peace, in acceptance and in Oneness."

For Pondering

The key to a clear and powerful awareness is the ability to approach every situation or event with a fresh, childlike perspective and with an openness to the possibilities that may be presenting themselves to you. Opportunities for growth keep arising in life. If we are asleep and not aware, we miss the opportunities and continue down the path of sleep, repetition, and possible creation of negative karma.

People who are asleep continue to buffer themselves from reality behind walls of 'what they know', which in truth is a recording that keeps playing in self-talk. This is the main reason why people avoid change like the plague, because change presents new knowledge or information for them to absorb. But, alas, they are more comfortable with 'what they are familiar with; with what they believe they 'know'.

So, to emerge from the *closed loop* of 'what you know' open yourself to new situations that contain new opportunities for experience and growth!

Contemplative Prayer

O God help me to remain open in each moment so that I do not let opportunities for new knowledge pass me by. Keep me as a child in your Light and your Love for I am your creation. I will awaken continually in each moment and shall reach the point of permanent awakening in your Oneness. I shall BE one with you and a co-creator of the Universe.

Meditation

Go inside and enter into the silence of your Being. Feel yourself as a child exploring a world totally new to you. As you venture inward, allow yourself the luxury of not knowing the world you live in. Allow yourself the exploration and discovery your inner world without naming anything or associating with any previous experiences. Stay with that for a while. When you return to your normal waking state continue to approach events, people, and situations with the same childlike, unknowing attitude. Do this especially with friends and relatives you are around frequently. Allow yourself to see something new in them. You will be amazed at what you discover!

Affirmation

I am a child of the Universe. I approach all of life with a fresh, open attitude which allows me to continually discover what I am meant to learn.

"Discern organizational and religious limitations that obstruct you from entering the inner kingdom"

CHAPTER 17

What is the best form for disseminating spiritual truths that will bring about the awakening of humanity? Organizations have overseen this process for thousands of years but have failed to sponsor awakening for individual members because the protection of the organization has been their prime concern. Religious and spiritual institutions appear to be unable to free humans from their worldly orientation and instead align with external objectives. In this chapter God explains how this happens and offers solutions to remedy the problem inspiring hope for the coming era. Listen to how this condition will be changed...

And God Whispered...

"Discern organizational and religious limitations that obstruct you from entering the inner kingdom. Religious and spiritual organizations have allowed the continuous teachings of my representatives on earth and have been a beacon of hope and light for many.

When religions have been suppressed, hopelessness and despair has arisen caused by the dominance of dark anti-human, anti-spiritual forces. A recent example of this has been communist governments in Russia and in other countries.

It is clear to anyone with conscious awareness that these systems were harmful to the spiritual progress of humanity. When suppression of religious or spiritual expression occurs, the inner freedom of the people is crushed and stifled. This has been a constant pattern for thousands of years under systems with different names but always working to take freedom from the people, causing great harm and obstruction to their spiritual growth.

There remains leaders today who have fallen prey to the dark forces and who plan to control the entire planet in the same way with a worldwide socialistic communist government. I will not allow them to succeed, and this will be the last time their action will be allowed since we are entering a new era.

A golden age of human growth and progress will occur that will be of interest to all sincere spiritual aspirants because there has existed a limited level of consciousness on earth with two camps, one moved by dark forces dedicated to dominance and control of people, and the other vested in spiritual principles, freedom and human spiritual growth. These two camps have been in battle for many centuries. Due to karmic actions throughout the ages those on the dark side have been more numerous and this has caused many souls to waste their lives chasing delusional desires while living completely under the dark influences until they finally learn to turn towards the light.

Religious organizations have not been entirely on the side of light since the dark forces have permeated every aspect of earthly life. What organizations purporting to represent me have done has been to block the expression of Spirit in the lives of their participants.

Once again... the expression of Spirit in the lives of many participants has been blocked by forming spiritual principles into dogmas and rules that limit growth and free expression.

This has also been accomplished through the appointment of certain people to guard the path to the inner kingdom. Organizational leaders decided what members of their organization should know and what they should not know and when they should be made aware of the inner spiritual information...if ever.

When one of my appointed teachers exits the earth leaving behind a core group of followers who take over the teaching that was left. Those given the responsibility to carry on the work are usually on a much lower level than the departed teacher. What happens is that they begin to step down the teaching to make it more acceptable to greater numbers of people. That is the first mistake.

Next, they begin to take control of the knowledge imparted by the teacher and decide what their members should know and what they should not know and how they should act in order to protect the organization. Essentially, they make decisions at the expense of the soulful spiritual expression of their members and the mission of the teacher.

A recent example is an organization founded by one of my sons who was given the mission to establish spiritual techniques for this era on earth. Those that were left in charge of the organization put in place changes that altered the teachings in an attempt to 'improve them'. These 'improvements' came from ordinary minds rather than from me...so the teachings were lowered considerably. This is how organizations operate when their founder passes over to the Celestial Realms.

The same was done by those who followed Jesus and other teachers I have sent, as a result, the world is in a state of spiritual confusion. Organizations thus, by virtue of their need to protect themselves, create a negative momentum that becomes difficult or impossible to change.

For this reason, in the coming new era, organizations will begin to fade away completely. Spiritual progress must take place on the individual level. Those who aspire to ascend spiritually will receive teachings directly from my fountain of Spirit facilitated by those more spiritually experienced.

At first, this will feel confusing, since humans are so used to following others, but I will ordain many of you as ministers and facilitators to assist others in reaching more deeply into themselves to reach their eternal Spirit.

As people gain more confidence in their own connection with me, they will leave the organizations and meet in informal small groups for fellowship, prayer, group meditation and reception of my blessing energy. I am pouring out these energies on the earth at this time to bring about a critical mass of awakened people, a tipping point.

When this occurs, others will spontaneously begin to receive my awakening energies and many, many people will begin to be transformed spontaneously. Then life on earth will change dramatically for the good. Organizations will fade away and spirituality will take a much more natural course as was my intention from the very beginning."

For Pondering

One huge asset of churches and organizations is that they offer scripture, spiritual works and reflections that help aspirants focus their minds and hearts on higher knowledge and truth. Unfortunately, many don't really 'listen' and 'feel' the content of what is presented to them.

Meditation organizations do offer techniques to go inside that are usually effective depending on the teacher, but the downside is that people identify with the organization and/or teacher and often lose their own sense of Self.

Connect what you hear or read in scripture with your inner experience. Ponder the truths that are presented to you. In this way you will be able to own and understand the wisdom of the ages.

The way to deal with this organizational trap is to always maintain a strong inner connection with YOUR TRUTH, with your own inner connection with the Divine. Then when you are venturing down one of these organizational detours, your inner Self will send you an intuitive message to put the brakes on. In fact, you will receive uneasy feelings anytime you are venturing into an area or situation that is a threat to your life mission.

Keep building a strong inner connection with Oneness and you will be guided in your life. That is exactly what created this book; 'And God Whispered…' I listened to the 'Whispers' within my Being from the Divine realm of Oneness and followed the guidance to share them with the world.

Contemplative Prayer

Help me Lord to remain open to your inner urging, guidance and teaching. I will draw close to those I feel are on a true inner path but will always regard your 'Whispers' that I receive as paramount in my journey so as not to be taken down spiritual detours created by others, who may be well-intentioned but who are in error. I will always pray for the discernment to know and 'feel' the difference between distortions and the truth.

Meditation

Go within to your quiet place and listen for any 'Whispers' that you hear. Sometimes they come through as 'feelings' or 'images.' Keep listening and feeling the Divine within your Self. Eventually you will receive your 'Whispers'. When you do, write them down and reflect on them to see what evolves from them in your life. Then stay open to further guidance that you may receive from your 'Whispers' experienced as intuitive inner feelings.

Affirmation

I am a Divine Being connected to the power and joy of the Universe. I can hear what the Divine guides me to hear and I can offer these 'Whispers' for others to hear to assist them on their journey into Oneness.

"I have looked into my churches and this is what I have seen…"

CHAPTER 18

What is the best way to approach spirituality? Religion, Meditation, a combination of both or an individual approach. A catalyst for energizing inner receptivity to the Divine is necessary. Religion offers an environment that allows one to approach God. Meditation groups usually follow a teacher or organization that was initiated by its founder. As an individual one may follow a path of spiritual exploration through reading scripture, or spiritual literature and adopting spiritual practices involving prayer and meditation, chanting, physical exercises and more. Most people who have been called to an inner path have received help along the way from their angels or guides so one is never alone. God provides guidance and advice on how one might proceed on their spiritual journey in the following 'Whispers':

And God Whispered…

"I have looked into churches, and this is what I have seen. Many souls have come to me through my churches, and many have been driven away from me because of my churches. Among those who lead and teach in my name include good and bad, positive, and negative as in all things on earth...a mixture of truth and untruth.

Yet there is a way to resolve the problem that exists in religion and get to the root of the difficulty, to shine light on it.

To throw out everything in religion would hurt many who are benefiting and at a point in their journey that requires a religious connection or expression.

To endorse everything in religion would also be wrong, for there are many faults that mislead aspirants who desire to come to me directly.

You may gauge the significance of religious practice for your own journey, however, and decide what you should do about your religious expression. Does your practice of religion lead you within your heart, or to a soul level connection with me? Does your religious practice cause confusion within you and lead you to guilt, shame or despair? Does your affiliation with religion primarily express a social or worldly focus?

Are your outward practices leading to a deeper desire to know me or are they creating greater separation from me and/or your fellow humans? These are the questions that will help you discern the viability of religious affiliation on your journey.

The purpose of religion is to bring you closer to me, to take you deeper within your Being so that you can experience the Oneness of all that is. However, because of the lower consciousness of those that often end up in control of religions the primary focus of religions has become external. The result is that participants get detoured into non-essential or distorted ideas.

A religion that lacks the ability to assist people in entering within their inner abode lacks validity. Such external and dogmatic organizations often exist for the egos of their leaders. To follow anyone's ego is to go deeper into the delusion of the world.

To truly make progress on the spiritual path, you must go within and find your connection with me. To do that you need to follow your Spirit.

Ego is distortion pure and simple and to be guided or impressed by another's ego is to be asleep in your consciousness. To awaken you must drink from the well of your Being.

Often, because humans live in their ordinary minds, which were designed to help organize their lives, they are easily entertained by ego ideas. Avoid the love of ideas and seek only the truth within yourself.

Many, because of their sleep, find the truth boring and too simple, yet the truth is rich and full of dimension. Truth must be pondered to be understood.

Don't be so easily taken off track by leaders immersed in the world. It is for this reason that worldly education is so revered, but education needs to be placed in the proper perspective. Worldly education is designed to keep you asleep. Stop seeking reinforcement from others as they will reinforce only what they see as important that proceeds from their worldly conditioning, from their sleep. Thus, you will be further confused and led into greater delusion.

Seek the deep understanding of the Spirit within along with my guidance and you will obtain spiritual growth and awakening from the world. Find others who have themselves gone within and have fellowship with them so that your internal dynamic will be automatically reinforced and you will discover more and more of the truth within your Being.

Seek the counsel of those who are truly wise as assessed by your discernment, for they will only wish for you to discover your truth. If you discover a religion that operates in this way, be with it. Religion that reflects inner truth in its outer practices and ritual is a treasure indeed.

Along with your external practices, follow the inner religion within your soul to find truth and journey back to me, back to Oneness, there we are One and from there you will be guided to your eternal home in me."

For Pondering

It all begins within your Being. Your connection to the Universe is through your Spirit. We are born into a material world, however, and often born into external religions. Until we become aware of our inner connection to the Universe, we can be deluded into believing that these religions and organizations carry the Truth and that we are subservient to them. However, no external religion or organization can override our internal connection to the Divine. When we discover that truth, we will never be detoured by ego driven organizations again. Some discover this reality earlier than others and become able to live independently from an early age. Others start later. It doesn't matter, eventually everyone gets there.

Once on the path of spiritual independence, one has the ability to become free and autonomous and continue on the true path of growth and spiritual development.

Contemplative Prayer

Beloved Oneness of the Universe assist me in taking the best of all my exposure to spirituality in life so that I may craft a journey directly to your presence and live within your constant blessings.

Meditation

Enter into the silence and peace of your Spirit. Feel the inner truth of your connection with the Divine. Meditate on the Oneness of All That Is and know that you are a part of that Oneness. Go back to that feeling of Oneness often during your daily activities. It is always present within you.

Affirmation

I am a vital conscious part of the Oneness of All That Is. All of reality passes through me and I through it. There is no separation, only Oneness.

"The one change that will change everything"

CHAPTER 19

The world is changing before our eyes, and we are the beneficiaries of a new way of practicing our humanness…a new way of Being. The energy that is now flooding the earth will enable us to better use our spiritual attributes which have formerly been submerged by material forces. These forces are destined to become obsolete and useless as more humans rise in consciousness and assist others in attaining Oneness. Let this very important chapter sink deeply within your Being:

And God Whispered…

"Your world and your life are about to change completely which will happen due to one change in the awareness of all people on earth. This is a result of the energy vibrations bombarding the planet at this time that is raising the vibratory level of human consciousness. Heavy material energies have kept human consciousness blocked from the awareness of truth and those able to use these energies most efficiently have risen to positions of power in all areas of life.

In government, religion, education, business, and even cultural endeavors the style and tempo of these leaders was domination and control keeping those not within their exclusive club in the dark as to their secrets of maintaining power thus engendering in 'ordinary people' misplaced trust as to their motives and intentions, in short…keeping the wool over their eyes.

Now all of this is beginning to change permanently as 'ordinary people' are obtaining the truth concerning all aspects of life and are being given the vibratory energy to become aware and understand the reality on earth. Within the Oneness awareness available to all conscious beings exists the ability to see through the motivations of the power grabbers and transcend the delusionary influences of material energy. There have always been a few in every generation who have broken the bonds of material energy and have entered the light of Oneness consciousness.

Now, because of heightened spiritual energy saturating the earth and being offered directly to anyone seeking to enter the spiritual flow of the universe, the proliferation of finer energies is being internalized by more and more humans.

Thus, the level of consciousness on earth will rise substantially within a short period of time and the truth of the binding activities of all power controlling humans in all aspects of life will be known.

This one realization will cause mass non-cooperation that will lead to the complete toppling of structures that have existed for thousands of years which include education, religion, government, and business, ultimately leading to completely new lifestyles and ways of communal living.

This will not be the result of any current ego-driven movements such as socialism, capitalism, progressivism and the like, rather earth life will simply evolve into something completely new and different. Life will be simpler and ego dominance and control will eventually cease to exist.

In the new civilization, everyone will be completely equal, and poverty and war will cease to exist. Spirituality will be the main objective of life. All of this will occur because of this one realization – *'everyone is equal before me and the universe!'* No one is higher or more valuable than anyone else. Education, Wealth, Status, Talent, Position, will no longer create massive egos and elitism as whatever now causes some people to condescend to others will lose its power. Humility will become the greatest asset.

Those who have wealth will have the desire to share their wealth with everyone else or they will lose their wealth because the old ways will cease to be effective in conducting business. No matter, because money will become useless as society creates new ways of exchange whereby people will share their skills in return for food, shelter, and specialized training.

Money will therefore cease being the object of worship by the masses as this material age comes to an end. So, become One with the flow of spiritual nourishment being offered and become an instrument of a new world of peace, love, and harmony."

For Pondering

All life on earth is now in transition. The chaos that we are witnessing is because the old ways of the world are dying, and a new consciousness is arising. In twenty years, you will no longer recognize the world as it is today. In fact, the world is already vastly different than it was twenty years ago. Hold on to your hat, for tremendous changes are in the works. Those that have dominated and controlled the world are being exposed and new, more conscious humans are taking their place. Material focus is weakening, and spiritual orientation is replacing it. Be a part of the new humanity by following these 'Whispers' that will generate your own 'Whispers.' Learn to follow your inner guidance into a new life of joy, peace, and harmony. A life in Oneness.

Contemplative Prayer

O Great Light of Conscious Oneness assist me in always and everywhere being aware that I am connected to all humans and that my mission is to assist all others in rising to consciousness in you. Make my humility vast and all-encompassing so that I never feel better or superior to anyone but rather constantly know that we are all equal under your Oneness umbrella of love and light.

Meditation

Go inside and ask for guidance in your life. Know that it will eventually come to you and be your inner guiding force that will synergize with the new energy that is changing the world. Every day tap your inner guidance while carrying out your daily activities. Meditate on receiving guidance for as long as you like and continue the feeling of guidance throughout your day. *(Repeat the following Affirmation internally as you dive within your consciousness to set the inner expectation for guidance.)*

Affirmation

I am able to tap into the Divine Consciousness of the Universe and receive guidance in my life. I will honor what I receive and follow the guidance available to me from Spirit.

*"Everything you do...
do with a full heart"*

CHAPTER 20

Part of the condition of the world is a result of so many people doing, acting, living, and expressing themselves with a small part of their Being and without the endorsement of their heart. Joy is often buried underneath negativity and self-doubt. So much time, thought and conversation is focused on criticism. In this chapter God provides guidance on how to change this situation and thereby create a world of joy and harmony. Take these 'Whispers 'into your heart.

And God Whispered...

"Everything you do...do with a full heart, filled with joy. This will connect your Being to what you are doing or expressing.

Many accompany their expressions in life with negativity, doubt, limitation, reluctance, and constant complaining. As a result, they only use a small portion of their Spirit in what they express. The effects of their actions are therefore fraught with contradictions. I will advise you on how to improve your expressions:

Stop complaining about everything; Stop doubting your effectiveness; Stop the constant negative dialogue with yourself and others; Stop joyless expressions of yourself; Stop limiting your actions to selfish motives; Open yourself up to possibilities.

Give freely and happily to others from your Divine nature. Fill your every thought, every word, and every action with your heart's endorsement. Love who you are and add what you can give to the world...*YOU ARE SPECIAL!*

You are a co-creator of the Universe with me. Be, express and act like my divine partner. Life is joy and you are bliss within your essence. Know that your joyous expression will re-make the world into a place without suffering.

Dominance and violence will disappear from the earth as more beings find and express their Oneness with me, and in Oneness, you truly realize that when you hurt others you are hurting yourself, and when you lift others up you are filling yourself with grace and good will.

Be my emissary of joy, compassion, and kindness. Let others know how much I love them through your love for them. Express your love and wield it with joy and power ...the power of Oneness."

For Pondering

Often people involved in spiritual movements and practices have a negative bias against the heart. They believe that 'emotion' is a lower ability in the human psyche and inferior to the 'mind'. Nothing could be further from the truth. Emotion needs to join with the mind and provide a dual power to the human psyche...emotion gives power to the mind. Additionally, when a human opens himself/herself up to love, incredible changes can occur. Love could not exist without emotion and its deeper counterpart, intuitive inner feeling. Allow yourself to feel, and more importantly, to express your feelings. When you do you will see tremendous inner changes. When you express your feelings, you will be less likely to present yourself as one who is aloof and does not care about others.

Contemplative Prayer

Divine Creator, flood me with positive energy so that it may submerge any negativity and criticism that I may hold in my heart and mind. Help me to always see the positive side of every issue so that I may be a force for good in the world. Assist me in becoming a warrior for positive change.

Meditation

Enter your silence and feel your inner peace. Know that your intuition is the way you will interact when you leave this life. Learn to feel it and use it here and now. Allow your intuition to speak to you and provide you guidance. Express gratitude for your intuitive ability to the Divine. *(Use the following Affirmation as a mantra during this meditation)*

Affirmation

I am an intuitive Being of Divine Nature. I will trust my intuition in all dealings with life and follow the guidance I receive through my Divine intuition.

"Stop the chatter...learn to live in the quiet recesses of your Being"

CHAPTER 21

In this chapter a touching story demonstrates the consciousness in which most humans live and the ideal consciousness that will bring about Oneness. A consciousness of quiet coupled with a sincere desire to feel God's presence.

And God Whispered...

"Stop the chatter...learn to live in the quiet recesses of your Being.

Let me share a story with you. Recently I decided to come to earth unseen to everyone including awakened humans and those with spiritual gifts. I arranged it that if a being was quiet enough, he or she would be able to feel my presence.

This is what happened... I entered a church and dwelled in the minds and hearts of those in attendance. Surely there would be someone there who could feel my presence. The internal mental chatter was so loud that I could barely feel my own presence. Their minds and hearts were filled with everything from internal complaints, criticisms, doubts, and fears to anger and negative wishes towards others. Mostly, there was a churning of daily activities; past and anticipated and so much to do with money and things desired.

Verbal and mental prayers abounded, but without sincerity and feeling, mostly mechanical and empty prayers. Ego thoughts, delusional and distracting, were prominent.

In the rear corner of the church however, sat a young woman who opened her heart to me. She desired nothing but to feel me within her heart. She was what I was seeking so I let her feel my presence.

She surrendered totally to me and gave herself to me, wishing to serve in any way I desired. She recognized that she was my child and that I would guide her life. With my presence, I ordained her to bless others. I will allow the secrets of the universe to flow through her Being so that she may share them with others. She will be one of my undercover saints appearing ordinary to others but having the power of my presence within her to bless them.

Every person has this potential, but it must be activated by the sincere desire to live in my presence and to experience Oneness with me."

For Pondering

People talk too much! What a waste of energy. Learn to talk less and live in your Being more, which doesn't require talking. Chatter, chatter, chatter... usually about desires for things of the world; the approval or disapproval of others; judgements and criticisms; likes and dislikes; ego inflation, etc. The mind needs constant entertainment and all varieties of experiences. Become sober and constant, proceeding on your journey through life to growth and spiritual development. When you decide to do that, the chatter will begin to become boring to you and you will choose a quieter way of being. There may be a tug of war in the beginning, but if you persist in honoring your inner life, you will win over the nonsensical chatter of the world. Eventually, you will walk around doing your daily activities and carrying out your responsibilities in a permanent state of inner connection with the Universe. Use this book as your doorway to reach and achieve that permanent state of Oneness.

Contemplative Prayer

Beloved Presence of All That Is, bring me to the quiet place of my inner Self so that I may feel with your blessing energy within me. I desire to enter a consciousness of Oneness in which I will live throughout eternity continually being a source of light and love to others.

Meditation

Enter your silence and feel your Being. Imagine that you are sitting in a church as the woman in the story was. Feel the desire to experience the presence of God and, to be able to always keep God's presence with you. Feel God's response to you and his blessing. Know that you are making strides in reaching Oneness consciousness that will be your permanent state. Accept and flow with Oneness and feel the appreciation God is giving you for being a sincere spiritual aspirant. Stay with the joy of that feeling for as long as you like...

Affirmation

I live in the silent state of my Being and in so doing prepare myself for the ultimate immersion in the Spirit of the Universe as light, love, and Oneness.

"This Dialogue Will Continue"

CHAPTER 22

In this last chapter, God promises to continue this dialogue in future volumes but also states that 'you have enough within these pages to formulate your mission to achieve Oneness and to become a minister of Oneness to others'. Reading and feeling the 'Whispers' is the first step. Spiritual practices are also necessary for you to develop your consciousness into a spiritual consciousness rather than a worldly consciousness of delusion and earthly desires. Specific techniques for enhancing spiritual awareness will be provided at the end of this book. Now listen to the concluding 'Whispers':

And God Whispered...

"This dialogue with you will continue until I am satisfied that I have given you what you need to accelerate your growth and liberation from the delusion and limitation of earthly existence.

More volumes will follow this first one, but you have been given, in this short work, many of the essential truths that can help you free your consciousness from the boundaries of limited earthly life. You now have the tools to begin pondering your existence as a child of light, one of mine. Fear not; rather open yourself to your true nature. Live in my Oneness and love one another. Help others grow. Form groups to study and reflect on the truths I have given you.

Know that the Spirit within you is unlimited, and that you are a unique version of me living and expressing your special talents and gifts, learning to love your brothers and sisters, and helping them on their journey.

Know that your meaning exists in the love you hold in your heart. All other expressions can flow from that love. Live in the Oneness of my being which incorporates all that exists in the universe.

In that Oneness open yourself to my son Jesus and other great ones that I have sent, to the Saints and Sages that have worked tirelessly to bring you closer to me.

Remain open to my 'Whispers' within yourself that will guide you and help you on your journey home. These 'Whispers' will help connect you to your own guidance so that you will reach the point of complete liberation from external expressions of the world and live in your own truth which is one with me.

My dialogue with you will continue in this form in other volumes and in the form of your own 'Whispers' that will guide you home to Oneness.

And so, it begins…"

For Pondering

The planet is currently at a major turning point in consciousness. We are on the brink of breaking through thousands of years of dominance, corruption and warfare that has absorbed the vast amount of energy available to allow many individuals to reach freedom from sleep and enter Oneness. Now it seems that the world is about to split apart as the elite power mongers on the planet are working to take over control of everyone's lives. They will not succeed because the power of love and consciousness is becoming stronger and stronger and winning many battles behind the scenes that will never be publicized. Yet here we are at the brink of the final battle that will bring on the beginning of a new age of spiritual freedom.

A new generation of humans is coming up who have tremendous spiritual gifts to offer. This book was written for anyone who is ready to embark on their spiritual journey and especially for this new generation which is yet another wave of advanced beings... many waves will follow. There are imbedded in these pages many triggering mechanisms from the universe that can be of great help to any sincere spiritual aspirant, who will be led to other triggering books as well. Let us keep our eyes and ears open to recognize the new leaders of the age and continue working on our evolution, which is the main task at hand. As nice as it is to consider what is happening on a large scale; the focus needs to be on what is being provided to you through this book. With it, you have tools for your personal work on your evolution towards Oneness. Enjoy the journey.

Contemplative Prayer

Beloved Heavenly Father, Jesus Christ and Saints of all religions assist me in becoming what I am meant to be. Help me to discover my personal mission in life so that I may visualize it and bring it into being. I am a worker in the spiritual vineyard of the Universe desiring only to create a new world of peace, love, and harmony. I am One with all that is good and blissful.

Meditation

Start with a half hour of Chapter 8 Meditation or another Meditation that you found special. Follow by sitting in silence. Envision a new world based on spiritual principles and that you are teaching and guiding others on their path. Allow yourself to feel cosmic energy entering through the top of your head and radiating out to your students. You are a source of power and love to everyone around you. Stay with the feeling of that reality for as long as it feels real to you. Then bring yourself back to your normal everyday consciousness. Do this meditation often while adding more experiences that you create in this new reality. By envisioning in this way, you are bringing the new reality into being and attracting experiences in your life that will take you there. Always listen for the 'Whispers' that come to you in meditation and in your normal waking consciousness. Do this same Envisioning meditation as often as possible with your eyes open. *(as in Chapter 12)*

Affirmation

I am a tool for the new consciousness arising on the earth. I will bring my Oneness to others in a gentle and loving way, always respecting their individual journey. I am One with the Universe. I am Love. I am Joy. I am Peace.

*A Seven Week Process
For Spiritual Awakening*

How to Use the 'Whispers'
To Establish Your Spiritual Life in Oneness

Once you have allowed the 'Whispers' to flow through your Being with several readings of the book, you will be ready to begin regular spiritual practices that will create the necessary changes within you to bring about Oneness Consciousness. The energy of the 'Whispers' is very powerful, yet subtle. The 'Whispers' merge with your personal energy field to soften and eventually eradicate the coarser energy you have absorbed from the world.

Several readings is only a suggestion. Take as many readings as you like until you feel ready for more specific practices that will address patterns you have formed in life that strengthen the worldly influences within you. This is your choice however, for if you would simply like to continue allowing the 'Whispers' to do their work within you…that is a valid approach. Many people though, will want to go further, deeper, and faster to achieve their Oneness connection with the Universe.

When, and if, you feel ready to move on you will need to become aware of the patterns and states of consciousness generated by them that magnify worldly influences in your psyche to become free of them. In fact, until you are aware of these consciousness traps you will have no desire to alter them because you will not have been paying attention to them. Awareness is always the starting point of spiritual life and the 'Whispers' will make you aware of certain conditions in life as well as the many pitfalls of a worldly orientation.

With this beginning of awareness, you can proceed to observe your own consciousness in specific ways that are provided in the Seven-week process. The spiritual practices will help you work on some major consciousness blockages and traps that keep you asleep.

When we form our ego/personality, we devise ways to deal with the world. It is formed from our many interactions with others from our childhood to the present time. What our ego/personality becomes depends on our personal essence deep inside and the ego/personalities around us with whom we interact during our early development and following life experience. Thus, environment is a strong tool for the shaping of our personal characteristics and our responses to life.

If the ego/personalities around us tended to be negative and critical we would develop responses to protect ourselves from being hurt emotionally. In this scenario we could become introverted with low feelings of self-worth or negative, aggressive, and dominant in our manner of dealing with others to compensate for our emotional injuries.

If those around us have been kind and uplifting in their interactions with us, we would be more likely be highly self-valuing and positive in our attitude toward life. In dealing with others, we would tend to be uplifting, positive and helpful with strong feelings of self-worth.

There are as many variations of ego/personality as there are individual people. We therefore will not focus on specific traits or patterns but will concentrate on the work of discovering how our own ego/personality works and what we might need to address to grow spiritually. The main characteristic of ego/personality is that in all variations there exists a feeling of separation, separation from others, separation from God and separation from the

Universe. The focus of our spiritual work is to remove or greatly diminish this feeling of separation in order to achieve Oneness.

Next, we need to identify certain aspects of our personality that may be limiting the emergence of our true Self within, our essence. To grow spiritually, we need to re-connect with our original essence and allow it to emerge into our ego/personality so as to soften and adjust the way we are with others and the way in which we perceive the Universe. Our essence is our true Self and will eventually take over who we are automatically once brought out our depths. When our Self is in operation it will diminish the feelings of separation from our ego/personality within our consciousness little by little until we are able to live in Oneness.

Here are some major patterns that we could observe in our ego/personality. In relation to our habitual nature, how robotic have we become? Can we override our habit patterns with our consciousness or are we totally asleep in our habits, obsessively doing what our machine-like habits dictate? This is the area where most people need to begin. In the spiritual practices suggested later you will be given specific ways to counter your robotic nature.

Do you talk too much? Do you have the need to be constantly talking about what you know, what you like, what bothers you, or what disturbs you about others? Excessive talking is a sign of low self-worth. You can observe yourself as you go through your day by gently watching yourself without judgement. If excessive talking is one of your patterns, there will be ways to counter the behavior so that you can become quieter inside. The thing is, that if you do talk incessantly; it is likely that your mind is also running constantly blocking your ability to meditate and become inwardly quiet.

How do you identify with the world? Identification is one of the chief faults that block your way to Oneness. Identification is when you place your conscious energy into something outside of yourself such as a material object or a car, a house, a piece of jewelry, an article of clothing, or in a role such as a wealthy person, a poor person, a dramatic person, one who knows everything, or a powerful person. The variations of objects and roles are endless, but the main characteristic of identification is that we put our personal energy into something outside of ourselves.

We can even identify with others such as actors, singers, and politicians and feel as though we are them. We identify with them as ourselves. Observe this in your nature and you will be given practices that can free you from the identifications you may have imbedded in your psyche.

One of the biggest obstructions to connecting with your internal life is the fact that most people on the planet are 'human doings' rather than human beings. People are doing, doing, doing and are lost in their activity, asleep in their constant going from one thing to another in their life. For such people, life becomes a blur of actions that leads to nothing worthwhile. When people die having lived this way, their experience in the afterlife is dull and confusing. Having lived in a blur they exist in a kind of fog when they leave the earth.

People need to learn to BE; to be able to feel their inner life and consciousness. To do this, they must make time to sit in the silence and 'feel' the Universe, to listen for God's 'Whispers', to explore their inner landscapes, to become spiritual. There has been a great deal shared about this in the "For Pondering, Contemplative Prayer, Meditation and Affirmation' sections at the end of each chapter. More will be provided in the Spiritual Practices section so that you can set the baseline for spiritual growth within yourself. Spirituality begins with the ability to BE.

Other problematic traits you might have could be negativity, criticalness, living in your mind, the inability to empathize with others, the inability to love, the inability to admit you are wrong about anything, or the need to control and dominate. The variations again are endless. Simply observe yourself objectively, non-judgmentally and your consciousness will eventually show you where you are on these issues and other issues that you may become aware of. Then you will be given insight into what to change and how to change it. You will find help from Spiritual Practices offered each week and from the 'Whispers'.

The idea is to become free from obstructions and blockages to consciousness and learn to live in your Being rather than in your ego/personality, your mind, your body, and your emotions all of which reinforce the feeling that you are separate from others, separate from God and separate from the Universe. Your Being is open to others, open to God and open to the Universe. Once you live in your Being you can eventually live in Oneness permanently.

Seven Week Process For Spiritual Awakening

Week One: Observe Yourself Objectively

During this first week the objective is to observe how you conduct your life, how you interact with others, the feelings that arise within you, the self-talk you engage in, whether you are negative or positive and anything else that you feel is significant within your ego/personality or in general the way you are. It is important not to judge or be critical of yourself in this process but rather to objectively observe. You will have plenty of time to evaluate what you see and may eventually decide to work on some things to improve your relationship to life. This is your spiritual work. Be gentle and kind to yourself. Much of what you have in your personality proceeds from responses to the world that you have formed in your youth and young adulthood.

Begin with this Prayer: Thank you dear God for placing me in the observation seat of my life. Help me to see what I need to see to carry out my spiritual work. Let me see through your eyes so that I can be objective and kind to myself as you are kind to me. I will put forward the effort necessary to split my awareness between my outward view that I use to deal with life and my inward view that I use to observe myself and my interactions with life.

Meditation: Choose a meditation at the end of the Introduction, Chapter 1 or Chapter 2. Use your chosen meditation at least once a day for the entire week. If you desire to have two meditations per day that is acceptable. The focus however should be on the specific Spiritual Practice for the week.

Spiritual Practice: You will be working at self-observation every day throughout the week. Begin on a Monday and end on a Sunday evening. Begin every day with the above prayer slowly and with feeling, speaking directly to God. Then go about your day. Get yourself ready for work if you work outside of your home or get your children ready for school... whatever is normal for you.

As you do what you do, observe how you do it as well as thoughts and feelings you have while doing it. You will likely forget about your self-observation often so gently bring yourself back to it. Check yourself at the top of each hour as a checkpoint. Go through your entire day and before you go to sleep write down anything you feel was significant in your observations, thoughts, or feelings during your day.

You could keep a seven-week Journal if you so desire, it will be beneficial for your spiritual work. Keep your reflections private for these are from the inner workings of your consciousness Here are some helpful suggestions:

> Observe exactly how you do things such as getting dressed, preparing food, eating, doing your job.
> Observe the tone of your voice with your significant other, with your children, with your pets.
> Observe your emotional reactions to others or in relation to yourself - do you see self-doubt

and insecurity, or do you see confidence and assertiveness, (just observe don't judge) do you see the desire to dominate and control others or the tendency to be controlled or dominated?
> Observe happiness and joy as well as sadness and discouragement.
> What do you tell yourself? Is your self-talk positive or negative? Do you put yourself down or assert yourself internally? Are you always criticizing others or are you more likely to notice their abilities and goodness?
> Check your attitude about everything. Do you have a superior attitude to others over money or position or knowledge? Do you lean on your separateness, or do you feel empathy with others? Are you gender superior or inferior or do you see others as equal to you as persons regardless of gender? Is your attitude mostly positive or mostly negative?
> Observe your habits and just how robotic they may be. You will be using what you learn about your habitual nature in week two.

You are beginning a process of self-observation this week that will help you to see what has been mostly outside of your awareness until now. As you continue to look at yourself in this special way without attempting to change things…the mere observation of your actions, feelings, thoughts, and attitudes will automatically bring about positive change. This process is similar to an actor or television personality that begins a show and watches recordings of themselves. They will begin to automatically make subtle changes in their intonations and expressions that improve their presentation. Feedback creates change.

This is the first week of your seven-week process. As you move on to other weeks you will be focusing on other aspects of your ego/personality. On Friday of each week, you could go back to prior weeks as a review. Self-observation will be a practice that you can employ for many years until you reach complete freedom in Oneness. At that point it will only be necessary to live in your Being, in your Spirit, and in the Presence of God.

Readings for the week: *Read the 'Whispers' from Chapter 2, Chapter 11, Chapter 13, Chapter 16, Chapter 21 (Read each chapter's 'Whispers' slowly three times feeling God speaking directly to you, one chapter per day. Repeat chapters as needed.)*

Affirmation: *(Repeat Affirmations aloud first, then more quietly, then as a whisper, then silently within.)*

I am a conscious being. Because of this I can use my consciousness to observe how I live my life and interact with others. What I see enriches my spiritual journey and assists me in awakening my potential as a child of God.

Week Two: Embrace Change

During your second week you will be focusing on your habitual nature and its mechanical, robotic ways. Hopefully you will have observed some of your habits in week one so that you can use these observations in week two. Here are some habits to work with:

> Personal hygiene habits
> Getting dressed
> Preparing food
> Eating food and drinking liquids
> Driving
> Work habits
> Chores around the house habits
> Parenting
> Taking care of elderly parents
> Care for your pets
> Other habits you become aware of

The purpose of this week's spiritual practices is to intervene slightly in your habitual nature so that you can become less a slave of the tyrannical aspects of our human condition. You will be intentionally inserting changes in order to increase your awareness of the way you are. You cannot do away with habits because they are imprinted in your psyche and useful for your life, but you can soften the effect they have on you. *OCD (obsessive compulsive disorder) people should skip this spiritual practice.*

Begin with this Prayer: Beloved God, Heavenly Father help me to live spontaneously and creatively in every way. Life is a portrait so let me be the artist that makes it always fresh and new, not a repetitive drumbeat that is constantly the same. In this way I can become a co-creator of the Universe with you in the way that you create. While you do use universal laws, you apply them differently in new occasions. Thank you for teaching me how to be this way in my life. Amen

Meditation: Choose a meditation at the end of the Introduction, Chapter 1 or Chapter 2. Use your chosen meditation at least once a day for the entire week. If you desire to have two meditations per day that is acceptable. The focus however should be on the specific Spiritual Practice for the week.

Spiritual Practice: This week you will be taking some actions to help you become less robotic in your habits and increase your spontaneous creativity. The idea is to add changes to the way you do some things. Proceed slowly and gently so that your continuity with life events will not be disturbed.

The order in which we do things is a part of our habitual patterns. In personal hygiene for instance the activities might likely be; brushing your teeth, taking a shower, drying your hair, putting makeup on, getting dressed, pressing clothing, and so on. Not too many changes in sequence can be inserted with these except possibly; brushing teeth and pressing clothing. But one possibility might be to change the time you awaken to different times daily during the week. Just do something a little differently than you do every day and observe how you react internally to it. Be creative and you will find other ways to insert changes in your routine. Keep in mind that this exercise is for one week and afterwards only occasionally to basically show your habits that you are in charge.

If you are a parent of small children, you are already making changes constantly and have probably had to deal with household chaos on occasion. Don't impose this exercise on your children. You can find changes to insert when you have alone time.

Getting dressed is an easy one. Simply find clothes that you don't normally wear and put them on. Observe how you feel.

Preparing food: find new recipes and make different types of ethnic foods, change it up a bit.

You can change your eating and drinking habits by either slowing down or speeding up your consumption of food or liquids. You will immediately become aware of the difference.

Driving…simply change your habitual route to various locations or the sequence in which you run your errands.

You get the idea. During this week you are going to insert changes in the way you do everything without creating major problems for your lifestyle. Observe yourself during and after these alterations to see what you feel and think about how strong your habitual nature is. I choose to do things differently all the time naturally because I do not want to feel like a robot. I now enjoy this technique after many years of experimenting with it and feeling free of my habitual nature which I allow to have its way when necessary.

Readings for the week: *Read the 'Whispers' from Chapter 1, Chapter 4, Chapter 8, Chapter 10, Chapter 19, (Read each chapter's 'Whispers' slowly three times feeling God* speaking directly to you, one chapter per day. Repeat chapters as needed.)

Affirmation: *(Repeat Affirmations aloud first, then more quietly, then as a whisper, then silently within.)*
I am free from the driving force of my habits and refuse to become robotic in any way. I will embrace newness and freshness in everything I do, say and think so that the product of my activities will not become dull or boring. I give my consciousness permission to be keenly aware of everything that I engage in on my journey through life. I refuse to fall asleep in my habits.

Week Three: Talk Less Listen More

In general, people talk too much! Incessant talking wastes spiritual energy and often keeps one's mind and heart engaged in superficial things that are not beneficial. During this week the objective is to discuss only things that matter or are important to life, work or relationships.

How can we distinguish between useless talk and discussion that serves a purpose? Observe your conversations and pay attention to your ego motives such as feeling smarter or wealthier than the person you are speaking with or whether you are seeking approval or aligning with complaints or negativity. How life oriented is your conversation? Will what you are talking about make a difference in your life or the other person's life?

Begin with this Prayer: Beloved God and my spiritual Father, help me to observe how I communicate with others and feel the content of their concerns so that I may minister more effectively to their spiritual needs. Help me to use my intuition more in order to understand others more completely. Help me also to deeply listen to what they wish to share.

Meditation: Choose a meditation at the end of the Introduction, Chapter 1 or Chapter 2 or the walking meditation after Chapter 11. Use your chosen meditation at least once a day for the entire week. If you desire to have two meditations per day that is acceptable. The focus however should be on the specific Spiritual Practice for the week.

Spiritual Practice: On day one of your week, observe your conversations without judgement or attempts to make changes. Then on the following days, ever so gently, work on talking less and listening more. As you listen, work on responding to the concerns and doubts others are having and counter with encouragement and positivity. Turn negative statements into positive responses.

For example, if someone says, "I never have any luck." Respond with, "what about that new job you received in March? I consider that pretty lucky." You get the idea, just find positive things to say. There is always something positive you can find. Turn the negative into positive.

If your positive turnarounds aren't accepted after several attempts, say something positive about your own life, then move on. Mainly, learn to listen more and try to feel empathetically what others are feeling. This is the key to building your intuitive perception which will serve you greatly in this life and even after you leave the earth.

So, work on talking less and listening more all week long. Learn that you do not have to respond to everything someone says. If topics are in uncomfortable areas, such as putting someone else down or gossiping; don't respond. Do not participate in conversations with which you are not comfortable. That is your right.

Keep these important points in mind:

> Work at not speaking ill of anyone.
> Speak only kindly and considerately.
> Listen and feel what others are expressing.
> Respond to the feeling content of what others say not to complaints or negativity.
> As you employ these strategies you will automatically talk less.
> Observe how much of conversation is negative.
> By talking less, you are preserving spiritual energy for its proper use.
> After this week of speaking less and adjusting the content of your conversations you will eventually reach a permanent awareness of how you speak with others.
> Habitual talk will diminish and awareness of your conversations will increase.
> This is a powerful and worthwhile practice in awareness and energy conservation.

After years of using this practice, it has become second nature to me. I listen to others deeply and respond positively as recommended above and find also that I talk about what others are interested in (only in acceptable areas for me) which makes people feel that they are being acknowledged and listened to. This is an excellent way to connect with others and build friendships.

After doing this for a while I usually come up with a spiritual comment on what was discussed so that they can depart with something useful for their life.

This is a life-changing spiritual practice.

Readings for the Week: *Read the 'Whispers' from the Introduction, Chapter 3, Chapter 5, Chapter 7, Chapter 9 and Chapter 22 (Read each chapter's 'Whispers' slowly three times feeling God speaking directly to you, one chapter per day. Repeat chapters as needed.)*

Affirmation: *(Repeat Affirmations aloud first, then more quietly, then as a whisper, then silently within.)*
I am aware of everything I do, think and say and I will only engage in meaningful conversations with others so as to keep my spiritual focus, preserve my energy and uplift those I come in contact with. Help me to always be aware of my positive focus on life and speak to others as you would speak to them.

Week Four: Turn the Negative into the Positive

Negative energy depletes the soul, brings about negative consequences in life, creates emotional turmoil, attracts negative events and is destructive to everyone it touches. We already touched on negativity in last week's spiritual practice, but there is much more to examine.

This week's practice will deal with negative thoughts and feelings, negative self-talk and the doom and gloom scenarios we often fall into.

There is a myth that operates in human civilization that states, "Unless you are critical you are not intelligent." People take this as license to criticize everything all the time and this alone creates massive negativity in the world.

Begin with this Prayer: Divine Presence within me and Spiritual Helpers around me, assist me in becoming aware of the ways I am negative. Help me to turn these around so that I may become more positive, more encouraging to others and more tuned into the positive nature of my Being. I will endeavor to become the positive person I was meant to be. Amen

Meditation: Choose a meditation at the end of the Introduction, or the walking meditation after Chapter 11. Use your chosen meditation at least once a day for the entire week. If you desire to have two meditations per day that is acceptable. The focus however should be on the specific Spiritual Practice for the week.

Spiritual Practice: On the first day of week four you should carefully observe how you may be expressing negativity; how you are casting negative energy on your experiences and interactions with others; and the extent to which you are negatively interpreting what is going on in the world. Watch but do not react or intervene with what you observe. Pay particular attention to the self-talk that you engage in... conversations with yourself.

As you enter your second day through the last day of your week you will work on intervention with your thought processes and self-talk to modify your negative feelings and inner reactions to events and to others.

Here are some *pointers* for your work on negativity:

> Remember that you always have a choice on how to react to events and situations
> You can frame a situation negatively, positively or neutrally... Example: Your boss tells you that you have a new position which is in effect a demotion. How do you react?

   1) A negative reaction might be that you feel insulted and somewhat depressed with low self-worth thoughts and thoughts of resigning or moving on.
   2) A positive internal response could be that you look at the change as a challenge and possible opportunity for growth in the company and exude a positive attitude about it all
   3) A neutral response would be that you take a wait and see attitude and evaluate on a day-by-day basis the result of the new position. Neutral is always somewhat positive since you resolve to objectively watch the situation giving yourself options and choices along the way. Often this is the best way to deal with events. It could be called the potentially positive approach.

> Learn to negotiate with your thoughts: If you find yourself thinking negatively about yourself or a

situation, think it through. Give yourself some more positive perspectives and allow positive thinking to work through the situation. Your emotions will follow your thoughts so don't allow anxious and depressing feelings to rule you.

> Speak to your feelings. You can say, "Everything is ok, I will find my way through this and come out feeling good about myself." or, "I always end up ok and on solid ground when I meet adversity, I can handle anything."
> Create self-talk *mantras* that you can use constantly: Pick one or two a day and chant them internally at the top of every hour.

Self-talk positive mantras:
a) *I am completely and utterly positive and exude positivity to everyone around me.*
b) *I always can overcome no matter what happens*
c) *In every adversity there is an opportunity.*
d) *I approve of myself and don't seek approval from others.*
e) *I have the power within me to overcome obstructions.*
f) *I will meet every challenge with the power of my inner self and my will to succeed in personal growth.*
g) *I reject all negativity and work to formulate positive responses to all events and situations.*
h) *I have the right to be my own advocate in all events.*
i) *I will be persistent in making my way through life always endeavoring to be calmly positive.*

j) When in doubt I will dive within my Divine Self for answers.
k) I am my own best friend and supporter.
l) I will intuitively perceive the intentions of others so that I can react appropriately.
m) I will respond to the negative statements of others' with positive encouragement.

> Always reject what is false and embrace the truth.
> Understand that all people are equally children of God and that education, wealth or position do not make a person superior in any way. These attributes provide opportunities to serve others not to rule others.
> Negative energy comes from the darkness... Positive energy comes from the light.

During your week you will have ample opportunities to work with the *pointers* given above. Select from one to three of them to work on each day in addition to the *mantras* you choose to use. This is the beginning of a lifetime of working on becoming more positive and seeking to diminish negativity. Negativity can be very subtle in the way it inserts itself, so a huge part of this practice is to become 'aware' of negativity. This focused week is, for many, the beginning of the quest for your true Self which is naturally positive.

Readings for the Week: Read the 'Whispers' from Chapter 6, Chapter 12, Chapter 18, Chapter 19 and Chapter 20 (Read each chapter's 'Whispers' slowly three *times feeling God speaking directly to you, one chapter per day. Repeat chapters as needed.)*

Affirmation: *(Repeat Affirmations aloud first, then more quietly, then as a whisper, then silently within.)* I am positive and self-affirming. I am kind and encouraging to others. I always seek to find the positive truth within myself.

Week Five: Follow the Flow of Your Spirit

The single most telling feature of living spiritually is the ability to follow inner urgings no matter what your programmed life approach has dictated. This is the ability to make changes as a result of prompting from Spirit no matter what. With Spirit there is no plan... just flow. Spirit is totally creative in the way it leads us forward in our spiritual life.

Following the flow goes against the rigid orchestrations of worldly planning. With the world there is a goal and a plan to achieve it. Sometimes that's a good thing, but if Spirit says no, go this other way, then there is a choice. Do we follow Spirit, or do we follow the plan?

Begin with this Prayer: Beloved God and Divine Spirit within, assist me in discerning the urgings implanted within me from birth that will lead me to awakening in you. My life is an extension of your divine wish for the Universe that you have given to all conscious beings. Help me to realize the fullness of Spirit within my consciousness. I am a co-creator with you of all that exists in my life because of your guidance and command. I am the extension of your divine hand in the world.

Meditation: Choose a meditation at the end of Chapter 1 or the walking meditation after Chapter 11. Use your chosen meditation at least once a day for the entire week. If you desire to have two meditations per day that is acceptable. The focus however should be on the specific Spiritual Practice for the week.

Spiritual Practice: On day one of this week begin with the meditation after Chapter 1 first thing in the morning. At the end of your session (at least 15 minutes or more) pose these questions to your inner self. 1) How have you urged me to follow my Spirit early in life? Sit in the silence and wait for an answer. If you do not receive one then, go on with your day. Often the answers will come to you later in the day or in a dream.

Meditate a second time in the afternoon with the walking meditation after Chapter 11. Ask yourself the next question:2) How have you urged me to follow my Spirit as a teenager? Wait once again for the answer.

The third meditation should take place early evening or before bedtime. Make this one at least a half hour session and use the meditation after Chapter 1 again. Follow up with question 3) How have you urged me to follow my Spirit recently? Sit in the silence and wait for an answer.

You will receive answers at some point. Jot down answers that come to you in your notes. Reflect on what you receive and feel how you were affected by the urges you were given.

Observe your activities during the rest of the week looking for times that you are presented with a choice to follow your daily routine or to follow Spirit. Be patient. You will get feedback from your inner life and you will learn how to follow the flow from Spirit.

Meditate at least once a day with one of the questions for the rest of the week. More times if you like. During the last three days of the week ask: What does Spirit want me to observe now? Is there another direction that I should consider in my life? Where is my spiritual flow leading me?

Readings for the Week: Read the 'Whispers' from Chapter 11, Chapter 13, Chapter 14, Chapter 15, and Chapter 17 (Read each chapter's 'Whispers' slowly three times feeling God speaking directly to you, one chapter per day. Repeat chapters as needed.)

Affirmation: *(Repeat Affirmations aloud first, then more quietly, then as a whisper, then silently within.)* I live in my Spirit which is not imprisoned by timelines dictated by the world. I am open to the urging impulses that Spirit provides that will often have me change direction and adopt previously opposed views on situations in my life. I flow with the divine guidance provided to me from Spirit. I can take a new direction as I am guided. My ego/personality does not impede my Spirit.

Week Six: Find Your Soul Expression

Everyone has one or several soul expressions that they need to activate. A soul expression is a special gift or talent that we have from birth. Many times, we have buried it within ourselves until it pushes its way out. It must be expressed on some level, or we will suffer from its stagnation.

Usually there are small indications early in life that give us a hint of the existence of a soul expression we have within us. For me, I always liked singing when I was a youth. When I sang, I felt a power coming from inside of me. But life caused me to bury singing beneath other activities that I focused on, such as work, dating and school. We are constantly making choices where to put our energy.

In my twenties I decided to learn guitar. As I learned to play and accompany myself, I re-connected a bit with my singing expression. For many years, I played and sang along with my children. It was great fun but something inside of me told me I needed to do much more.

Several years later I received internal tugs prompting me to join a choir. Since I wasn't involved in church at the time, I dismissed these urges. Finally, I became involved in a church group and joined the choir. Soon after, the parish decided to have cantors or song leaders and I became one. That's when my soul expression kicked in. I was hooked. I scheduled myself as cantor in five different churches and led singing three or four times a weekend.

My next step was to accept a position as a music director and choir leader in a parish. The momentum of letting a soul expression out is so powerful that it leads to many opportunities for its use. Many, many musical expressions have occurred since then including producing 12 albums for CD and digital release. My soul expression for singing has been activated and will be used for as long as I am able to sing and play guitar.

One of my other soul expressions is writing and this book clearly speaks to that expression.

Begin with this Prayer: Beloved God assist me in discovering the soul expression(s) that you wish me to bring out into the world. These are your gifts that we need to honor and use so that your world will be enhanced and blessed by the talents that you provide. Thank you for your care of our souls and for implanting your gifts within us.

Meditation: Choose a meditation at the end of Chapter 14 or the walking meditation after Chapter 11. Use your chosen meditation at least once a day for the entire week. If you desire to have two or three meditations per day, better yet. The focus however should be on the specific Spiritual Practice for the week.

Spiritual Practice: There are countless activities in human life on planet earth. Painting, sculpting, crafting, gardening, landscaping, cooking, baking, exercising, running, weightlifting, practicing martial arts, singing, dancing, playing an instrument, composing music, marketing, advertising, selling, managing, driving, customizing cars, card making, stamping, quilt making, practicing religion, swimming and diving to name a few. Any of these and many others could become someone's soul expression, although mostly these are often done quite superficially. A soul expression fully engaged is done with one's whole Being.

How to discover your soul expression(s): Reflect on your life experiences regarding expressions in music, art, athletics, religion, spirituality, business, science, wherever you have been led to explore interests. Place notes in your journal or notebook on what you have discovered.

Choose the one expression that seems to give you the most joy and meditate on it seeking to discover how deeply it goes within you. Then choose another expression that might be a soul expression and meditate on it later in the day. Take notes on what you found.

If you feel that you already know what your main soul expression is, either through the above process or because you have had strong feelings about it prior to this week's exploration, review what you have done about using it. Decide what further actions you might take to expand your current use of it.

Continue throughout the week to reflect and explore your relationship to your soul expression and to meditate once or more daily it. During the last two days sketch out a plan of how to further develop your expression in your life. Visualize positive experiences of soul expressions in the future.

Be sure to begin your reviews and meditations with the prayer and affirmation from this chapter each time. You will strengthen your resolve to express your soul expression as you practice the process in this chapter. Many blessings on your search. This is very important to your spiritual development.

Readings for the Week *Read the 'Whispers' from Chapter 20, Chapter 8, Chapter 15, Chapter 13 and Chapter 10 (Read each chapter's 'Whispers' slowly three times* *feeling God speaking directly to you, one chapter per day. Repeat chapters as needed.)*

Affirmation: *(Repeat Affirmations aloud first, then more quietly, then as a whisper, then silently within.)* My soul is endowed by God with talents, skills and abilities that need to be discovered and expressed if I am to enter fully into the realization of Oneness. My soul expression not only helps to fulfill my life purpose but adds beauty and joy to the world. My soul expression is an essential aspect of my Being.

Week Seven: Work on Being

Most humans live in their ego/personality. It is currently the way of the world. In the new spiritual world that is forming and arising, this will change. Your work this week will bring about the change within you and you can spread it to others.

The ego/personality is formed and shaped beginning early in life as the child interacts with those around him or her. He seeks to feel pleasant and safe and avoids feeling pain and insecurity. Those around him/her such as parents, relatives and siblings having been already shaped in their ego/personalities will work to condition the child in the same way they were conditioned.

Usually, they work to crush internal impulses coming from essence in the child such as the desire to have their own way or their spontaneous activity such as dancing or spinning around the room or speaking in unknown languages. In effect, older, more powerful people will wear down the impulses of the child and teach him or her to have a false personality adapted to accepted behaviors in the world. It is a false personality because it is conditioned in them and often goes against their natural internal impulses and instincts.

This ego/personality is thus superficial and can lie or become devious or dominate others. Everyone is different in how they form their personality, but the ultimate truth is that most people will need to re-build a relationship with their inner Self and entire Being if they are to make spiritual progress. To grow spiritually, one needs to become aware of and 'feel' one's Being which includes the inner Self or essence and ego/personality. This week we will focus on Being.

Begin with this Prayer: Heavenly Father, Divine Mother, as the parents of my Being help me to re-connect with what I came into life with... with my inner Self. Assist me in consciously feeling all that I am in my Being so that I may continue on my path to Oneness in you. I am your spiritual child and desire to grow spiritually in my life here on earth and afterwards when I join you in the heavens.

Meditation: Choose a meditation at the end of Chapter 14 or the walking meditation after Chapter 11 or any other meditation you like in the book. Use your chosen meditation at least once a day for the entire week. If you desire to have two meditations per day that is acceptable. The focus however should be on the specific Spiritual Practice for the week.

Spiritual Practice: Practice this Conscious Being exercise called Morning Sitting every day throughout the week. It replaces your regular meditation in the morning. You may add one or two suggested meditation sessions in the afternoon and evening before sleep. The walking meditation is recommended for the afternoon session.

Morning Sitting: Sit in the morning in a relaxing chair or recliner. (Relax – do not use meditation postures or worry about a straight spine. This is an alternative to meditation) Feel your Being, feel God's presence within you, feel Spiritual Helpers, Angels, and Saints around you. Feel yourself vibrating in Oneness and feeling joyful and full of life potential. Feel a very light and fine energy within and around you.

This week you will be concentrating on internal conscious exercises totally. You are working on 'feeling' your Being. Do not become frustrated if you do not feel your Being at first. Keep using your Spiritual Practice, Prayer and Affirmation. You will have the experience of your Being arising within you all of a sudden, while you are doing some work or cutting the grass or driving down the road. The objective is to turn your gaze inward and 'feel' the reality of your spiritual existence as a Being. Once it begins it will become second nature to you so be patient with yourself.

When you can 'feel' your Being, the experience of Oneness (or feeling a part of everything in the Universe) is the natural next step in your work on consciousness. Enjoy your practice.

Readings for the Week: *Read the 'Whispers' from The Introduction Chapter 3, Chapter 13, Chapter 14, Chapter*

22 and the Epilogue. (Read each chapter's 'Whispers' slowly three times feeling God speaking directly to you, one chapter per day. Repeat chapters as needed.)

Affirmation: *(Repeat Affirmations aloud first, then more quietly, then as a whisper, then silently within.)* I am a child of the Universe imbued with the spiritual attributes necessary to attain Oneness with All That Is. I will achieve the awareness and inner feeling of my Being which holds all the potential given to me because of my spiritual heritage. I am a spiritual Being endowed with power to BE.

General Spiritual Practice: Cleansing Your Soul
(This powerful Spiritual Practice can be used anytime)

Reflect on your life asking God to help you replay events and experiences that 1) you feel badly about, 2) that taught you something valuable, or 3) for which you need forgiveness.

> Ask God for forgiveness and cleansing.
> Within your mind and heart ask the injured person for forgiveness.

For me this happens spontaneously. Events come to me (flow to me from Spirit) and I acknowledge them and feel the error made if there is one (or the blessing of a beneficial exchange). I allowed these memories to flow as they came and so I have been able to have feelings cleansed as requested. This is like starting your life review before you leave the earth… beginning to cleanse while still in the body. This process will assist you when you leave the earth and make you much lighter while living your life here.

SOME FINAL THOUGHTS

We are each on a spiritual journey working to understand our special place in the Universe. Beginning where we are, we journey to experiences that show us our unique footprint on the sands of time. Tuning into the deepest part of ourselves, we learn to expand into the Oneness of All That Is. The simplest way to begin is with the idea that each of us is special and unique, blessed with the potential for total realization of God and the Universe. Let us journey then...

Closing Prayer

Heavenly Father, Beloved God, Oneness of the Universe... I am grateful for your 'Whispers' given to the world through this book. Assist me in entering the inner kingdom that you provided to each of us and taught by Jesus to his direct disciples. Help me to know, feel and understand all that you offer to us through your 'Whispers'. Help me to hear your 'Whispers' directly within my Being and to radiate your love to everyone I meet. I am eternally grateful to be your child, please guide me throughout eternity to my home in Oneness! Amen.

www.ingramcontent.com/pod-product-compliance
Lightning Source LLC
LaVergne TN
LVHW041708070526
838199LV00045B/1258